dreams and their interpretation

Dr Francis A. Menezes is well known in the field of management education and applied behavioural science. He is Director of Turiya, Centre for Creative Solutions. Prior to this, he was Director of the Tata Management Training Centre for 27 years and Director of the Tata Administrative Service. Dr Menezes is the Founder-Director of the Indian Association for the Study of Dreams (IASD) and was elected to the Board of the IASD in 1985. He pioneered 'Creativity and Dream Workshops' in corporate training in India and has worked with the dreams of managers, public administrators, entrepreneurs, religious groups and many others. He has presented papers on his work with dreams at IASD annual conferences in the United States, at science seminars in India and at the Global Management Development Forum in Barcelona, Spain. Dr Menezes, who was a member of the boards of Indian Airlines and Tata-McGraw Hill, received Pune's Pride Award for Excellence in the World of Academics in 1997.

dreams and their interpretation

Other Lotus Titles

Arjan Singh	*Arjan Singh's Tiger Book*
Ruskin Bond	*The Green Book*
Indira Menon	*The Madras Quartet: Women in Karnatak Music*
Jagdish Chander Wadhawan	*Manto Naama: The Life of Saadat Hasan Manto*
Jeannine Auboyer	*Buddha*
John Lall	*Begam Samru: Fading Portrait in a Gilded Frame*
Lord Meghnad Desai	*Nehru's Hero, Dilip Kumar in the Life of India*
Maj. Gen. (Dr.) R.M.Kharb	*Dog Care*
Maj. Gen. Ian Cardozo	*Param Vir: Our Heroes in Battle*
Namita Gokhale	*Mountain Echoes: Reminiscences of Kumaoni Women*
Neelima Dalmia Adhar	*Father Dearest: The Life and Times of R.K. Dalmia*
Nina Epton	*Beloved Empress: Mumtaz Mahal*
Rachel Dwyer	*Yash Chopra: Fifty Years in Indian Cinema*
Ralph Russell	*The Famous Ghalib*
Rashna Imhasly-Gandhi	*Psychology of Love: Wisdom of Indian Mythology*
Savita Devi	*Maa . . . Siddheshwari*
Sumati Mutatkar	*Shrikrishna Narayan Ratanjankar 'Sujan'*

Forthcoming Made Easy Titles

Shalini Advani	*Single Parenting*
Ramya Sreeperumbudur, Smita Barooah	*Pregnancy Facts*

Other Forthcoming Lotus Titles

Duff Hart-Davis	*Honorary Tiger: The Life of 'Billy' Arjan Singh*
John Lall	*Taj Mahal & the Glory of Mughal Agra*

dreams and their interpretation made easy

Dr Francis A. Menezes

LOTUS COLLECTION
ROLI BOOKS

Lotus Collection

This edition published in 2005
The Lotus Collection
An imprint of
Roli Books Pvt Ltd
M-75, G.K. II Market
New Delhi 110 048
Phones: ++91 (011) 2921 2271, 2921 2782
2921 0886, Fax: ++91 (011) 2921 7185
E-mail: roli@vsnl.com; Website: rolibooks.com

Also at
Varanasi, Agra, Jaipur and the Netherlands

Editor : Nandita Jaishankar
Cover : Arati Subramanyam
Layout : Narendra Shahi

ISBN: 81-7436-353-X
Rs. 195

Typeset in Fairfield LH Light by Roli Books Pvt Ltd.
Printed at Samrat Offset, B-88, Okhala, Phase-II, New Delhi

TO MY WIFE CORA, AND MY CHILDREN

URMILA AND GIRISH

WHO BELIEVE IN THEIR DREAMS,

AND TO MONICA

WHO MADE IT HAPPEN.

Contents

Acknowledgements

My earliest involvement with dreamwork was via the Gestalt route. Pope John XXIII had brought about a whole new, open environment in the Church and a great deal of experimentation was going on. In the early '80s, my Spanish Jesuit friends, Jaime Filella, who retired recently as Director, ESADE the Business School in Barcelona, and Oriol Pujol who was then head of Seva Niketan, a social service organization, were active as catalysts in the transformation process. They invited me to lead several encounter groups, where I used Gestalt dreamwork when the occasion arose. With affection, encouragement and support they launched me (unknowingly!) into the fascinating world of dreams. My interest though, was in Management Training, and I thought the cathartic aspects of Gestalt would not be acceptable in the management classroom. I had already founded the Indian Society for Applied Behavioural Science in 1972 with a group of friends. But it seemed to me that T-Group Training was rather limited and superficial. I was searching for an effective and acceptable training method for personal growth programmes.

During these initial years, Audrey Wilson (now Pillay) worked closely with me. We introduced Creativity and Dream Workshops at the Tata Management Training Centre, in Pune, India. They soon became part of the regular Training Schedule. Audrey shared with me a great deal of the skepticism and criticism coming from all around. 'What do dreams have to do with Management?' Plenty, according to this book! It took a couple of years before those who had come to scoff stayed on. I feel privileged to have worked with Audrey. She has a very special gift with dreams. She approaches the dreamer with a caring and sensitivity that is rare.

My friend and colleague of close to 40 years, Ronjona Mukarji, certainly played an important part in keeping my interest in dreams going. We spent months in the early years recording each other's dreams of the same night, not missing out even the minutest details such as 'cough... yawn...scratches her head...frowns...' a recording machine would miss. She has painstakingly read the typescript of this book and has made valuable sugestions. Ronjona served for many years on the Board of the Indian Association for the Study of Dreams.

In 1985, I read about the Second Annual Conference of the International Association for the Study of Dreams (ASD) and wrote to the President of the Association, Robert Van de

Castle, asking him if I could attend. There was quick reply in the affirmative. It was great meeting Bob and attending his workshop. By a strange coincidence, ('There are no coincidences', says my Guru) I was staying with my brother who works for the World Bank, and lives in Vienna, Virginia in the same neighbourhood as Rita Dwyer—a dynamic force in ASD. Rita took me under her wing and literally drove me to the conference at the University of Virginia. Rita was a nuclear scientist whose serious accident in her laboratory had appeared to a colleague in a precognitive dream. Rita has held every single conceivable executive position in ASD and has contributed greatly to its growth. She is active to this day. She was mainly responsible for my being elected to the board of ASD for a term. This year she invited me to join a panel on '*Dreaming Our Futures*' at the June Conference of ASD in Denmark, but my doctors did not think it would be wise for me to travel right then. I truly owe her a lot. Including an apology for not making it to Copenhagen!

By another coincidence, on my way to Virginia in June 1985, I stayed with another brother at Scarsdale, outside New York. I discovered Montague Ullman lived close by and called on him. We talked, and he presented me with his book, *Working with Dreams*, with a warm and encouraging inscription, which is one of my most treasured possessions. Monte Ullman was quick to respond to my request for permission to present his approach to dreamwork in this book.

I am also an unabashed admirer of Gale Delaney for her prolific writing, for the insightful way she works with dreams and for her vibrant personality. We had a memorable lunch at Santa Fe on her birthday just before she made a presentation to the ASD Conference, 1993. Her methods and techniques are practical and easy to follow. We often use her methods in our dream groups.

Patricia Garfield, whose book *The Healing Power of Dreams* is an international best seller and dominates the Internet, willingly and warmly gave permission to use excerpts from her book. Ann Sayre Wiseman, an old friend who knows India well, not only gave her permission but also sent me the updated version of her popular *Guide to Working with Dreams.* Jayne Gackenbach spent a couple of days at my Centre in Pune and spoke to the members of the Indian Association for the Study of Dreams about her work at a special seminar. Eric Craig and I became instant friends, and we talked a lot. It was he who introduced me to Medard Boss, whose work is referred to in this book.

The Osho Commune at Pune provided me with a great deal of space and freedom to experiment. Many of Osho's disciples from all over world, and especially therapists from Easlen, worked with me individually or in groups, helping me to hone my skills and to give me the wide cross-cultural experience I sought. Ma Dwari, a German therapist and close friend, is planning a book based on the dreamwork she has done with me. Devendra has helped to get the permission to use the excerpt from Osho.

The Indian Association for the Study of Dreams was the vehicle through which we reached many people. Sangeeta Jethmalani organized several meetings and the experiment with Colorpuncture which is described in the book. There are many members of the Association and my dream groups, too numerous to mention, who have shared their time and dreams to make this book possible. Shirin Captain, Krishna Jhunjhunwala, Shobana Haldar, Sukanya Patwardhan and Punam Gupta especially come to mind. My former secretary, Muriel Christy, helped a great deal with the first typescript. A dream enthusiast, she has worked effectively with her own dreams and made many changes in her life.

It will be difficult to mention all the corporations where I have conducted 'Creativity and Dream Workshops', and still do. But I have to record the debt I owe Dr Subroto Ganguly who, as chairman of a large public sector corporation, was the first to take the risk of letting me use dreamwork in an organization development effort with the 32 scientists of his Research and Developement Centre. Fortunately, the experiement was successful!

My children have been more than curious about my work with dreams. My daughter Urmila attended a Dream Workshop with her husband John, who is a dental surgeon, and both felt it was a great experience. My son, who works in London, is a dream addict, and works a great deal with his dreams, sometimes even on e-mail!

Monica Drego came to a Dream Workshop a couple of years ago, quite distraught after the loss of both her parents in quick succession. She had a precognitive dream where her father sent her to me as a guide and showed her my picture long before she actually met me. Well, that is the stuff that dreams are made of! Our collaboration has been very fruitful. Monica made the dream book project her own and coaxed, cajoled and coerced me into completing it on schedule. Her enthusiasm never flagged. Her high energy seems endless. She provided the project all kinds of resources at all times, including her own dreams, inputs on the scientific aspects of dream laboratories and research on the references.

Finally, I must express my gratitude to my Guru, Ramesh Balsekar, for his blessings, and for his willing permission to use extracts from his work.

Introduction

When I was six years old, I was chosen to play Joseph the Dreamer in my school play. The teachers made such a fuss over me, that I must have decided then that it was a good business to be in. To this day, whenever I enter a bookshop, I head straight for the section that might have books on dreams. In India, it inevitably leads to a spot ensconced between the tomes on astrology and the paperbacks on palmistry. The books are profusely illustrated with no serious intent. That is why I was happy to seize upon the opportunity when asked to write a complete guide to dream interpretation. I have attempted to make this book as complete as for example, a guide to Chinese cooking, knowing fully well that some chef on the outskirts of Shanghai is secretly working on a new recipe for Beijing Duck!

The book follows a certain sequence, as if it were a journey, where the reader is taken by the hand and walked step by step through what at first, appears to be a mysterious universe. After a preliminary introduction to dreams and dreaming, he is given the tools of the trade. He is taught how to recall and record his dreams. To generate, as it were, the raw material for study and interpretation. This brings us to the critical part of the book—how to interpret dreams. And here is where the reader is introduced to seven different, practical ways devised by the leading dream psychologists and dream therapists of our time. As far as I am aware, there is no other book that covers such a large number of methods.

Another significant feature of the book is that having presented each method of interpreting dreams, I have shown how I have used them in practise in my work, mainly but not exclusively, with Indian participants. In the act of transition I may have deviated from the original intent of the pioneers, but being friends, I am sure they will forgive my transgressions. A major strength of the book is that it is a practitioner's guide. I have tried to make it simple for the reader to use each method.

Given the Indian penchant for rituals and the mysterious, which the West finds increasingly attractive, I have devoted a whole chapter to Incubation. It dates back to sixth century Greece and the Oracles at Delphi. I have described four methods including the one I have developed over the years with my colleagues, and which we find exceedingly effective.

A chapter has been devoted to what I have called a

rainbow of dream experiences. It is meant to satisfy the curiosity and quest of both casual and serious readers. The chapter covers the esoteric experience of telepathic, precognitive and past-life dreams. As well as messages received through dreams from dead relatives. In every case, actual examples are quoted from my dream groups. This is another salient contribution of the book.

Since I have worked in the corporate world for several years, managers and management education has been my special area of interest. Despite some initial resistance, we were able to introduce dreamwork in management training, and I am happy to say that to this day, leading corporations invite me to lead workshops for their managers. It is certainly not widespread, given the fact that there are very few people who can lead dream groups. Readers should find the managerial issues of power and powerlessness, women managers and job insecurity—familiar themes in their own lives and dreams.

A chapter has been devoted to nightmares. I have discussed the probable causes of nightmares and ways to deal with them, also pointing out the differences between nightmares and night terrors. Readers will find the chapter on the healing power of dreams very useful and fascinating. With her gracious permission, I have presented Patricia Garfield's Questionnaire which is an excellent diagnostic tool and very easy to use. Given the worldwide concern with health and healing, readers will be pleasantly surprised to discover that they carry a doctor within who is always on call.

The connection between dreams and creativity is an old one. Scientists, artists, designers and composers have often depended on their dreams for inspiration and answers. We discuss this experience in some detail, and explore the obstacles to creativity and overcoming them.

A unique feature of the book is the inclusion of the mystic experience of dreams and dreamless sleep. My colleagues in the West have told me that their study and interest ends with REM sleep. I hope the discussion in the final chapter of the book will kindle an interest in going further. For many of us in the East, dreams are the beginning of reality.

Pune FRANCIS A. MENEZES
October 2004

1

Exploring the World of Dreams

This book is an invitation to a journey like no other. It covers interstellar space, delves deep into the seven seas, and crosses rugged mountains and raging rivers. It is a journey that takes you to exotic forests and into deep ravines, through lush, green valleys and across endless tracts of desert sands. As you proceed, you will experience in explosive detail the vagaries of man's passions in times of war and in times of peace, during fires and floods, hurricanes and gentle showers. You will experience your own conflicts and your own moments of joy and despair. It will be an inexorable journey into the self—into the world of dreams!

But let us start from the very beginning, if there has been any beginning. And go to the very end, if there is going to be any end. A dream, like life itself, has neither a true beginning nor an absolute end. It is a continuous process, that goes on night after night, through your lifetime on this earth—and perhaps, for several lives afterwards—if one is to believe the mystics.

What is a Dream?

So, what is a dream? Is it a night-time fantasy? Or a tale told by an idiot, full of sound and fury, but signifying nothing? Is it the result of an undigested dinner? Or a vision—a series of pictures of events—that is presented to a person who is asleep? Is it a message from God? For, as the sacred book of the Jews, the *Talmud* says, 'an uninterpreted dream is like an unopened letter.'

Our dream life has a reality of its own. It is part of the business of living. During the day, we experience a 'waking reality' and as we fall asleep, we experience dreams. We are the same person—awake or asleep—despite the fact that we experience life differently in both these states. Sleep and dreaming takes care of two very important needs of our bodies—first, physical rest and second, to take care of our psychological, emotional and spiritual needs. Dreams perform several functions. They help to process and integrate the day's events and provide clues often in the form of metaphors, to help us solve some of our everyday problems. Dreams also help us in wish-fulfilment of our desires and goals. They assist in reviewing past events, reminding us of parallels in the present. They protect sleep by disguising stimuli such as anxieties that would otherwise awaken us. Dreams also have deeper functions—they provide pathways to recover repressed or forgotten memories, whether from childhood, infancy, in-utero or even past lives.

The American dream researcher, Calvin Hall (1966), offers the following definition: 'A dream is a succession of images, predominantly visual in quality, which are experienced during sleep.' Dreams are an integral part of sleep and essential for the healthy functioning of body, mind and spirit. A deeper insight into this phenomenon can enable us to learn to use the immense power of our dreams.

The fact that a dream is a succession of mental pictures accounts for finding that a dream occupies only a brief period of time, perhaps only a few seconds in many instances. A picture is very economical, since it manages to say a great deal in a short span of time. As Turgenev Hall, 1966, the great Russian novelist of the nineteenth century observed, 'a picture may instantly present what a book could set forth only in a hundred pages.'

Enter Sigmund Freud

Prior to Sigmund Freud's monumental study in 1899, *The Interpretation of Dreams (1976)*, European research into dreaming had been undertaken by isolated individuals like Alfred Maury, who experimented with the effect of physical sense impressions on dreams. Maury (1853) gave his famous example of the bed rail falling on his neck—an event which triggered off a long dream in which he dreamt that he was captured during the French Revolution, and of finally being led to the guillotine (Menezes 1989).

During this period, medicine was not interested in dreams, which were usually viewed to be meaningless hallucinations. It was against this background that Freud reacted. By studying his own dreams in detail, he evolved a theory of dreaming by which he understood dreams as the disguised fulfilment of the dreamer's infantile sexual needs. As most dreams were not overtly sexual, he maintained that the manifest dream, that is, the dream which one recalls, has already been censored by the mind, and that behind it is a latent dream to which it bears little resemblance. Freud concluded that the manifest dream needed to be disguised, so that its content would not shock the dreamer into waking. He thus believed that 'Dreams are the guardians of sleep and not its disturbers.' (Freud, 1976)

C.G. Jung and the Collective Unconscious

It is an apparent paradox of modern psychoanalysis that one of its key concepts was revealed to its founder C.G. Jung, in a dream. Jung was a devoted pupil of Sigmund Freud, but was uncomfortable with his teacher's insistence that every dream and neurosis had a sexual origin. Jung on the other hand, had greater spiritual insights in his work. The disagreements between the two led to the end of their personal and professional relationships.

In his revealing dream, Jung found himself on the second floor of a two-storey house which he did not recognize, but which he knew to be his own. The second storey comprised a comfortable salon elegantly furnished in a rococo style, and although Jung felt at ease here, he was restless to explore the ground floor. Descending the stairs, he discovered that the lower level was in complete contrast to the floor above. Here the tone was sombre, with floors of bare brick, and the furnishings were almost medieval in character. At the far end he reached a heavy door and on opening it, found a stairwell which led to a vaulted chamber that appeared to have been built in Roman times. There, in the semi-darkness, he saw a ring attached to one of the stone slabs and on pulling it, discovered narrow stone steps leading into a cave dug into the rock. Inside the cave, he discovered shards of bone and broken pottery, which he concluded must have been the remains of a primitive culture. Then, just as he was about to examine two human skulls, he awoke.

'It was plain to me that the house represented a kind of image of the psyche,' he later wrote in his autobiography, *Memories, Dreams, Reflections*, 'that is to say of my then state of consciousness, with hitherto unconscious additions. Consciousness was represented by the salon. It had an inhabitated atmosphere, in spite of its antiquated style. The ground floor for the first level of the unconscious. The deeper I went in, the more alien and dark the scene became. In the cave, I discovered the remains of a primitive culture, that is, the world of primitive man within myself—a world which can scarcely be reached or illuminated by consciousness. The primitive psyche of man borders on the life of the animal soul, just as the caves of prehistoric times were usually inhabitated by animals before men laid claim to them.'

From the images of his dream, Jung evolved the concept of the 'Collective Unconscious' which was a layer of the psyche that incorporated memories, instincts and experiences common to all humanity. Such patterns, which he felt were inherited, may manifest as dreams or mystical visions.

Dreams are composed of images that arise from a variety of sources. It is a popular belief that dreams are determined by somatic factors, such as the position of the dreamer's body, indigestion, fever, pain, and other physical stimuli, such as noise, light, cold, and heat. Jung acknowledged that some images are influenced (for example, a bell may be incorporated in the dream if an alarm clock rings), but he insisted that images are determined mainly otherwise, that is, physically.

Psychophysiological studies tend to support Jung's

conclusion. In a 1958 study by Dement and Wolpert, neither dreaming sleep nor dream images were produced by sounds, lights, and tactile stimulation presented to the dreamer during non-rapid eye movement (non-REM) sleep. Even during REM sleep, external stimuli had to be startling in order to have a marked effect on the content of the dreams that were occurring. A pure tone of a 1000 cycles per second was judged to be incorporated into and subsequently elicited dreams only 9 per cent of the time; a flashing 100 watt light, 23 per cent; and a spray of cold water on the sleeper's skin, 42 per cent. The awakening stimulus, a bell, was never incorporated into the dreams.

A source of dream images more prolific than physical stimuli during sleep is the dreamer's everyday environment. Jung mentioned, for example, that the dreamer's occupation appears frequently in dreams: a musician dreams of a performance, an architect of buildings, and a teacher of classrooms. No data seems to be available on the frequency of dreams depicting the dreamer's occupation, but the immediate environment of some dreamers or the laboratory in which the dream took place, was reflected in as many as 30 per cent of laboratory dreams, according to some studies.

The language of dreams, according to Jung, is at least as complex and varied as the language of consciousness. Dream language is made up largely of non-verbal images that vary in complexity and vividness more dramatically than corresponding waking experiences.

On a relatively simple level, dream language is often figurative, that is, akin to figures of speech. For example, in day-to-day conversations we may characterize a person to be a 'snake-in-the-grass', 'pig', or 'pussy-cat', to mean that he or she is perfidious, unmannerly, or gentle. Similarly, in a dream, the unconscious may use the image of a lion, the king of beasts, to characterize power. Sometimes the dream makes a pun, for instance, an image may depict 'pray' to suggest 'prey'.

On the next level of complexity is the metaphor. For example, a dream image of crossing a bridge can be a metaphor for making an important transition. The image of imprisonment likens the dreamer's situation to one of severe restriction. Thus, abstract thoughts are expressed through concrete imagery.

Some dreams contain images that are fantastic and even physically impossible, such as the dream of a 16-year-old boy in which he was being followed by the devil and where, in 'deathly terror, he leaps into the air and hangs there suspended'. Jung relished such picturesqueness in dream language. He found it more vivid than abstract statements because it is not limited by the conscious mind and can draw upon a greater wealth of associations.

Fritz Perls and Gestalt Dreamwork

Fritz Perls broke away in essential ways from both Freud and Jung, and is reluctant even to use the word 'interpretation' in his dream concepts. He is the third leg of the tripod that holds all the worthwhile theories and approaches to dreams and their interpretation.

Fritz Perls recognized that dreams use symbolic picture language, but was concerned with what this revealed about the dreamer and his problems, instead of treating it (as Freud did) as a disguise mechanism, whose purpose is to prevent the dreamer from understanding his dream.

He insisted (as Jung did) that any particular dream has reference to the dreamer's present life situation, as well as to his basic character structure formed by early childhood experiences. He looked for the dreams' 'existential message' in the here and now, and referred to the character-forming experiences of the past only incidentally.

He agreed with Jung that a dream should be interpreted in any manner the dreamer finds most useful. If it reveals what appears to be an unconscious infantile desire, this should be examined for how it affects the dreamer's life. On the other hand, Perls believed that dreams contain far more than mere wishes and that we should always look for their most relevant message, whatever that might be. His methods are simple and straightforward, and can be used by ordinary people at home to gain insight into personal problems and conflicts. They are not a specialized discipline to be used only by experts in the consulting room, nor are they concerned with the treatment of mental illness.

Freud, Jung and Perls are the firm tripod on which most dream theory and analysis rests. Most experts in dreamwork draw inspiration from one, or all three, for their work. There are a large number of psychologists who are specifically adherents of Jung and call themselves Jungians. Those who follow Fritz Perls are called Gestalt therapists.

The Advent of Dream Laboratories

With dream laboratories active in many parts of the world, there is now scientific evidence that everybody dreams every night, though few seem to recall their dreams in the morning. That is why people either dismiss their dreams as worthless, or simply believe that dreams are a great mystery beyond their understanding. It is possible to dream five different dreams and awaken in the morning forgetting them all! Even the ability to recall differs from person to person. Some people recall fragments as they move through the waking day. Others recall their dreams clearly, remembering each minor detail, including the colours, shapes, sounds and emotions. Apparently, those who are more inclined to use the right side of the brain (which controls the affective, emotional and artistic side) recall their dreams more vividly than those who are inclined to use the left side of the brain (which controls the logical, mathematical side). Yet, the interest in dreams is widespread. Although people are curious and fascinated with this phenomenon, at the same time inhibitions to ask questions exist, because a lot of material in dreams is personal, appears bizarre, or is viewed as frivolous.

The Dreaming Brain

Sleeping and dreaming are still poorly understood. Most dreams take place during the REM phase of sleep, when some parts of the brain are aroused, while others remain quiet.

In 1953, at the University of Chicago, in the Department of Physiology, Professor Nathaniel Kleitman and his student Eugene Aserinsky set up the first laboratory that would study (REM) during sleep through the use of several monitoring devices. The person being tested had electrodes attached to his face and scalp. The electrodes transmitted signals from the brain to the Electro Encephalogram (EEG) machine, which amplified them a million times so that they could be read. Similarly, electrodes placed near the eye, recorded the eye movement called Electro Occulogram (EOG) and so on. A detailed description of the dream laboratory and how it works is given later in this chapter. It is noted that respiration, heart rate and blood pressure are more elevated and irregular in

REM rather than non-REM. Oxygen consumption, brain temperature and cortical blood flow are increased in REM but decreased in non-REM. That is how we are aware that most of the dreaming occurs during the REM period of sleep, as if the person is watching a play being enacted in front of him.

The function of sleep has both psychological as well as biological benefits. Our brain is a chemical plant and the primary sleep-regulating brain mechanisms are bio-chemical in nature. It has been found that biogenic amines, in particular serotonin and catecholamine noradrenalin (also known as norepiniphrine), play an essential, if not exclusive, role in the regulation of sleep. They are found in heavy concentrations in various parts of the brain stem.

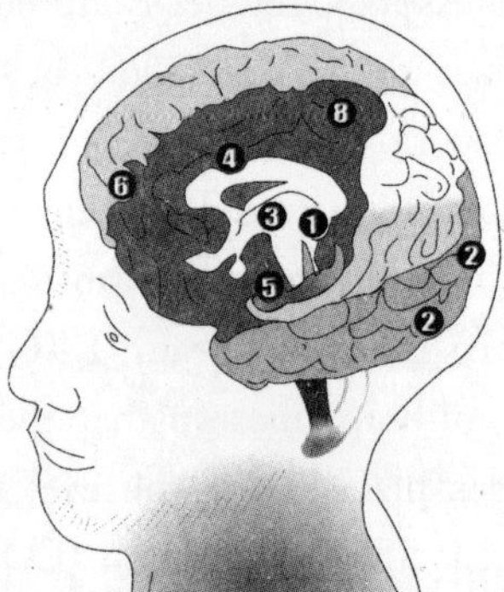

Source: *Walter Reed Sleep Laboratory, National Institute for Deafness and Other Communication Disorders.*

Active Areas	Inactive Areas
1. **Limbic system:** Creates strong emotions, aggression and long-term memory. Activity gives dreams emotional and sexual power. 2. **Extrastriate:** Processes complex visual patterns, such as faces. 3. **Thalamus:** Carries sensory signals to and from the cortex. 4. **Anterior cingulate:** Regu-lates motivation and curio-sity. May explain dreams' vivid imagery. 5. **Pons:** Triggers REM sleep by stimulating brain into activity.	6. **Prefrontal cortex:** Regulates intelligence, conscious thought. Inactivity may be why dreams are bizarre, illogical. 7. **Primary visual cortex:** Regulates vision when the person is awake. 8. **Inferior parietal lobe:** Processes experiences into memory. Dreams may be hard to remember because this part of the brain does not process them in the normal way.

Frequently Asked Questions

Here are a few frequently asked questions about dreams that I encounter in my work with individuals, groups, and corporations:

Does everyone dream every night?

Yes, everyone maintains a fairly regular sleep-cycle every night. In an eight-hour sleep, each sleep-cycle lasts for about

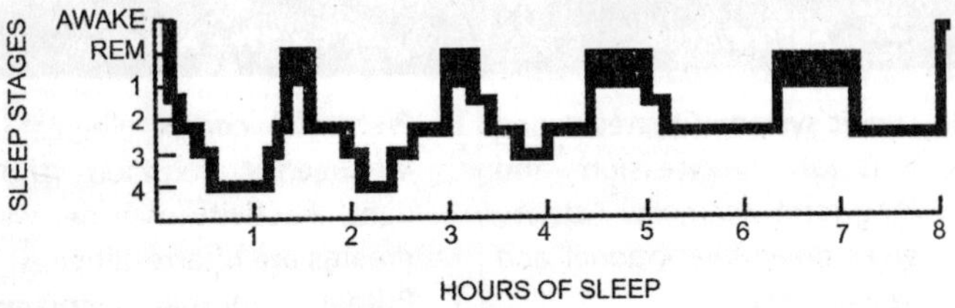

A typical night of sleep in a young adult.

90 minutes and goes through four stages, as illustrated above. The first period of dreaming occurs about 90 minutes after we fall asleep and lasts for about five to 10 minutes. Through the night, the dream periods become longer. The final dream just before a person awakens may last for up to 40 minutes. This dream state is called REM sleep because during this period, the eyes move rapidly under closed eyelids, as if the dreamer is watching a scene. The other period is called non-REM, which indicates that there are practically no dreams during this time.

Do animals dream?

Laboratory studies have indicated that all mammals, even opossums, which are so primitive that they are called 'living fossils', have the same sleep-cycle as humans, including dreaming. Of course, we do not know what they dream about—perhaps, food, sex, and power politics—like most human beings! Apparently, animals do experience imagery because they move their feet and whimper or growl as if they were awake.

Does everybody dream in colour?

Many people are convinced that they never dream in colour. However, modern research has proved otherwise. In dream laboratories, volunteers were questioned immediately after waking up from a REM period of sleep. They reported that they dreamt in colour on over 80 per cent of the occasions. Colour in dreams however, is rapidly forgotten, unless something specifically catches our attention, like a green tree or a red rose. In my work with hundreds of dreams, I discovered that black and white dreams often suggested the negative mood of the subject—for example, dreams of death or serious illness.

Do dreams solve problems and answer questions?

Indeed, they do. In fact, the main purpose of this book is to enable the reader to learn how to use dreams to heighten his awareness, to obtain a better understanding of his concerns and to find solutions to them. There is a great deal of evidence to show that at least some dreams in themselves, can significantly influence the course of the dreamer's life. The insights gained provide many opportunities for growth and change. The degree to which our dream life influences our daily life is to some extent determined by how we use our dreams. In the dream state, we seem more exploratory, more playful. We allow ourselves the freedom to experiment with different solutions to the problem and try to generate varied creative responses to our questions. In the dream state, we are freed from the constant distractions of daily life and stimuli that affect our senses. There is an absence of the censors that inhibit our thinking during the waking state.

Why do we repeat the same dreams?

Some people often have 'recurrent dreams'. There are two reasons why dreams repeat themselves. The first is that images and emotions connected with a particularly important event in the past recur when the dreamer faces a similar problem later in life. For example, a person who is very anxious about an exam may dream the previous evening that he has prepared himself for the wrong paper—history instead of mathematics. Then, at the age of 40, when he has to make an important presentation to his boss, the same feelings of anxiety could recur, triggering off the old exam dream of his youth.

The second reason why dreams recur is because the unconscious wants to reveal something important to the dreamer which he is ignoring or not ready to confront. The dream is, as it were, knocking at his door. For instance, a young man in one of my groups dreamt he was travelling in a suburban train at great speed, even though there was a red light in the distance and another train was approaching from opposite direction. Both the trains stop just in time. The driver of the oncoming train puts his head out of the window and shouts, 'Hey, what the hell are you doing?' I repeated the question in class. The young dreamer suddenly understood the dream. He exclaimed aloud, 'Sir, I'm marrying the wrong girl!' Apparently, he had been forced into the match even though he was engaged to another woman. The dream warned him and helped him to make the right choice.

Do blind people dream? What is the nature of their dreams?

Yes, blind people do have dreams. The kind of dreams they have depend on how long they have been blind, and whether they have been blind from birth. Where there has never been any visual input, there is no visual imagery. The well-known dream therapist Montague Ullman, points out that a blind person uses all of his other sensory modalities (touch, smell, hearing, sense of movement) to construct his dreaming experience. The perception of the dream environment as experienced through his other senses seems real to the blind dreamer. Helen Keller writes of 'seeing' in her dreams, much as she does when awake but, of course, with a much richer array of fantasy and imagination. For those individuals who are not blind from birth, visual imagery tends to diminish over time.

Are there dreams that come true?

There is a common belief that early morning dreams come true, but this is not based on any dependable evidence. The belief may be based on the fact, that just before waking up from the last cycle of sleep, we dream for the longest period of time—over 40 minutes. The dreams experienced early in the morning are therefore easier to recall. Since the unconscious has been 'cooking' the dream the entire night, it has much greater clarity in the early hours of the morning.

The kind of dreams that come true are called precognitive dreams. These dreams occur before the actual event, often as a warning to alert the dreamer. For example, the executive director of a large public sector corporation in Gujarat recorded a dream in one of my workshops, which detailed his death in a car accident almost a year before it actually happened.

The second type of dream which may be said to come true is the telepathic dream. It incorporates into the dreamer's account a truth about another person that he would have no way of knowing. For example, a woman in India dreamt that her son who lived in Boston had met with a serious accident and was in hospital. Her other children reassured her that they had spoken to him only a few hours ago, and that he was preparing to celebrate the Independence Day weekend with friends. The woman's dream turned out to be true. Soon after speaking to his family in India, the son had joined his friends on a trip to New York by car and had met with an accident on the way. The time of the accident and the mother's dream coincided. This is typical of a telepathic dream (see Chapter 5).

What does it mean, when in a dream, you realize you are dreaming?

Such experiences are called lucid dreams, because they are unusually vivid and also because the dreamer is aware during the dream that he is dreaming. Ann Faraday, the distinguished writer, says that she would rather accept the term 'dream of knowledge' for such dreams because it is a more suitably dramatic title for what is undoubtedly a dramatic phenomenon. An important conclusion that such dreams create, is that we have the power to change our dream world in ways which would be termed magical in our waking life. I remember a dream in which I was trapped inside a small cave and the water from the ocean flooded in, threatening to drown me. Fortunately, I turned lucid just in time to 'will' the waters back into the ocean, and to produce a boat to carry me safely to shore.

Therefore, in a fully lucid dream, we can use our awareness to change the dream in any way we choose. We can fly and soar like eagles. Meet a wise old friend or relative. Or sit back and watch the progress of the dream. There is a joyous quality to many lucid dreams that is irresistible. Everything in the dream is more real and vivid than in the waking state. If you hear music in the lucid dream it would probably be sweeter than any earthly sound you know!

Experiments conducted in dream laboratories at the Stanford University Medical Centre have shown that almost anybody can be taught how to become lucid in their dreams. Children are known to use such knowledge to deal with nightmares.

What about walking or talking in our sleep?

Both these activities have no direct relationship to dreaming. They occur during the non-REM or non-dreaming phase of sleep. Since they represent transitory releases of speech and motor mechanism, they may have more to do with extra motor energy in the body. It could possibly be the only way people who are repressed feel safe enough to express themselves. Incidentally, contrary to popular belief, a sleepwalker can injure himself.

What is a dream laboratory? How does it work?

Dreaming is a deeply personal experience. Initially, there were many myths surrounding dreams but in 1953, important discoveries were made by scientists that cleared many puzzling questions about dreams.

At the University of Chicago, in the Department of Physiology, a discovery was made quite by accident. Professor Nathaniel Kleitman, the world-famous expert on sleep, was conducting a series of experiments on the sleep of babies, when one of his students, Eugene Aserinsky, noted that an infant's eye moved rapidly and jerkily under closed lids for short periods during sleep. When he reported his findings to Kleitman, they decided to extend their study to the sleep of adults. To observe the eye movements directly during sleep would have been cumbersome, if not impossible. So, Aserinsky and Kleitman improved this method by monitoring sleep through proper devices. The person being tested had electrodes attached to his face and scalp. The wires leading from each electrode was plugged into a terminal box at the head of the bed, slightly above and behind the person.

The electrodes transmitted signals from the brain to the EEG machine which amplified them a million times, so that they were translated into a written record that could be read by the human eye. Similarly, electrodes placed near the eye recorded the eye movement called EOG. Muscles activities using the Electro Myogram (EMG) were similarly recorded. Other parameters, such as respiration, blood pressure and pulse rate were frequently recorded, but EEG, EOG and EMG (records usually taken from the chin) were essential for sleep stage measurement. Today, these procedures are routine and have been improved upon to obtain even more accurate results.

It is noted that respiration, heart rate or pulse, and blood pressure are more elevated and irregular during REM than non-REM sleep.

Oxygen consumption, brain temperature and cortical blood flow higher during the REM phase, but lower in the non-REM phase.

Penile erection, middle ear muscular activity, twitches of small facial muscles and limbs are all very common during REM but absent or rare in non-REM.

Thus, we can conclude that most of the dreaming occurs during the REM phase of sleep. It is almost as if the person is watching a play being enacted in front of him.

2

Easy Ways to Recall Your Dreams

The journey of a thousand miles begins with a single step. It is the same with our journey into the self, or into the world of dreams. The first step is dream recall. To remember a dream is part of the natural process. Though everybody dreams every night, few people actually recall their dreams—and there are good reasons why they do not.

Many reasons have been given by experts as to why most people cannot recall their dreams. A simple and obvious one is that people would rather not remember their dreams because they include content, such as events and memories, that they are not ready to face. There is also a certain amount of repression which inhibits dream recall. Freud was of the view that even when you do recall your dreams, the part of the dream which is not remembered is of more significance than that which is recalled. There is great truth in this statement.

People also experience dream deprivation if they are on substances or have taken certain prescribed medicines such as sleeping pills. The loss of a dream probably takes place just before waking up, or at the very moment of waking. Members of my dream groups are advised to lie absolutely still when they realize that they are awake, because even the slightest movement of the body can bring in a rush of waking thoughts—and the dream is lost.

The Four Characteristics of Dreams

To help recall a dream, it must be remembered that every dream has four characteristics:

- A setting
- Actors
- Action
- Feelings

A setting of a dream is the background, or the framework, within which the dreamer works his nightly art. A setting is extremely important for interpreting the dream. It provides innumerable clues as to what the dream is about. In India, we often find that dreams are set 'in my native village'. The dreamer goes back to his roots, or to the start of his life's journey, or is simply feeling nostalgic. Other common settings are the office, train, school, the market place or home. Curiously, but not surprisingly, many managers start their dream narration with, 'I am in a jungle ...' apparently referring to the organizational jungle. The way the setting is described by the dreamer tells you immediately how he perceives his workplace. People also dream about being in graveyards or at funerals. Death and dying are sometimes subjects of dreams. However, dream deaths could simply signify the end of a relationship, a project or an era. Dreams may be set in exotic places, palaces and pleasure islands. Or even in outer space—on Mars, for instance.

Next, there are actors in the dream. You may be one of them. For example, you may dream that you are walking with a friend in the park. Or you may not be a participant, rather, an observer. 'I am watching my father and uncle talking privately in the corner of the room…' or 'I see myself and a friend climbing up steep steps of a tall building…' There may be crowds of people, a mob, fellow-passengers on a train journey, or you may be alone—the only actor in your dream. The actors may also be animals. A young secretary dreamt that she was standing at the corner of a field and saw a wild bull chasing her boss. Not a difficult dream to interpret, is it?

Action is the third most important characteristic of a dream. The characters in your dream could be running, fighting, flying or simply lying down. Often, you may be performing mundane, daily tasks, like cooking, repairing things, watering plants, feeding the dog. Such dreams are usually classified as 'housekeeping' dreams. However, if the action is more vigorous, like cycling along a road, climbing a mountain, crossing a river in spate, boxing, flying, falling, or even making love, then the energy in the action, as well as the metaphors used in the dream, would suggest what the dream is trying to convey.

For example, an engineer, who was just not making progress on his project at work had this dream:

> I am cycling up the hill desperately trying to reach the factory on time. But, however hard I pedal, I keep slipping down back to the bottom of the hill ...

The fourth, and perhaps the most important, characteristic of a dream is feelings. Dreams are a right brain function, which is the affective part of the brain where feelings reside. While the left half of the brain is responsible for logical functions—facts, figures, formulae, sequential thinking and so on, the right brain is responsible for more creative aspects of our functioning, like artistic ability, musical ability, imagination, spatial ability and dreams (a detailed discussion on the left and right brain functions appears in Chapter 9).

A dream may have a single feeling running through it. For example, if a close friend has suddenly passed away, your dreams may be entirely suffused with a sense of loss and sadness as you relive old memories. The scene of the cremation may repeat itself endlessly, triggering off feelings of pain and sorrow. You may experience sadness as the dream unfolds in the beginning of the night and the same feeling could persist till you wake up in the morning and realize with surprise, that your pillow is wet.

To Kill a Cat

A dream may cover several emotions. Here is the dream of a senior scientist who worked in a research and development centre:

> I am sitting quietly in a room. Suddenly, I notice some small animals coming in. Two of them. They are jumping around. I get irritated so I kick them out of the room. Then, a black cat comes in, also very troublesome. I take hold of the cat and squeeze it and kill it. Immediately, through the window, I see the boss looking at me, very furious. He is very annoyed at me for killing the black cat. He likes the cat. Then, I think, he may try to kill me for revenge with a revolver or something ... but, I am not worried. I am quite cool. I laugh at him mockingly ...

This is quite an unusual dream. The dreamer has experienced a whole range of emotions—from being calm, to feeling angry, furious, revengeful, nonchalant and derisive—all in the space of one dream! Feelings expressed in the dream help a great deal in understanding the emotions experienced by the dreamer.

To recall your own dreams, whether in the middle of the night or early in the morning, you could use any, or all, of these four characteristics of the dream (setting, actors, action, feelings). A good technique is to catch the dream by the tail. Ask yourself, as you lie in bed, motionless, 'What was it that I was seeing? Where was I? What was the setting of the dream? Who were the people around? What were they doing? What am I feeling right now? What were my feelings during the dream?'. In other words, try and remember the setting, actors, action and feelings. Once one of the characteristics is pinned down, the entire dream will be easily recalled. You could then give the dream a title, as if it were a film or painting. The examples given earlier could be titled 'The Black Cat Dream', 'Sumati's Funeral', or 'Bull Chasing Boss' respectively.

Kitchen Hints to Aid Dream Recall

1. To make a few notes, you will need a pad and pen handy. This is the first step in ensuring that you will not lose the dream. Some experts suggest keeping a dream diary or journal. While this is good idea for a few months, in the long term, when you are learning to recall and interpret your dreams, it is better to record only the important ones.
2. Acquiring the right attitude towards your dreams is very important. If you try to force yourself to recall a dream,

not only will you disturb your sleep, you will wake up with a heavy head. Be gentle with yourself. You will remember the dream without any effort when you are ready. It helps to be patient.

3. Try and relax without drugs or sleeping pills when you go to bed. Research has shown that as you get more interested in dreamwork, you become more capable of dealing with your work problems and less dependent on crutches like drugs and alcohol. Listening to soothing music or reading a good book can help, as can taking a long walk or chatting with close friends or relatives. Some people advise drinking herbal tea. Others prefer meditation or reciting their favourite *mantras*. Try whatever suits you and fits into your routine. It must be effortless, and enable you to go to bed in a relaxed state.

4. Although you cannot force yourself to dream, or even to recall one, a silent request to your unconscious (your sleeping sage) to help you remember the dream, often helps. Make a soft decision almost like a prayer, to remember your dream in the morning. It is surprising how easy this becomes. The difficulty then will be not how to recall a dream, but which of the several dreams during the night you should record! Often, you may have a series of dreams in one night. Or, you

may have a series of dreams over a week, very much like a television serial. This could occur when the unconscious is exploring the dream in different ways until you are ready to look at the issue and deal with its solution.

5. Some people who do not recall their dreams are quite happy not to. They say that whenever they do remember a dream, it is usually an unpleasant, even scary one. Thus, pleasant dreams are quickly internalized and become part of the waking day. You simply are aware that you have been in a good mood since the time you woke up, not connecting it with the dreams you experienced at night. In fact most 'scary' dreams are not what they seem. For instance, there was a young man who was astounded to discover, after working on interpreting his dream, that his 'death' in the dream only indicated that he had got rid of a troublesome old behaviour pattern and now felt like a 'new' man.
6. As you become more proficient at observing your dream as it occurs, you will notice the tiny gap between the waking state and the onset of the dream state (the REM stage). You can almost hear a click. Modern dream experts ignore this gap, but ancient sages have pointed out that it is of great significance. This gap, they say, is our reality. It is the screen which is the background

against which the entire drama of life takes place. In deep sleep, the blank space becomes much more evident. Patanjali calls it, 'A taste of *samadhi* ...' (see Chapter 10).

7. Try and be natural about your sleep. Waking up to the harsh sound of an alarm clock may not be the best way to recall a dream. Wake up naturally and gently. It is easy to give yourself a mental wake-up call before you go to bed. Try to maintain regular patterns of sleeping and waking everyday. We live in times where a number of people actually believe that sleep is a waste of time. They feel guilty if they sleep for 'too long'. This kind of thinking is quite unfortunate, as a great deal of healing takes place naturally during sleep.
8. When you are experiencing emotional stress or work overload, you might appear to face dream deprivation. It is possible that the amount of dreaming remains the same, but the recall is difficult. You can rest assured that the unconscious has not abandoned you. It is working hard in the deep recesses of your mind on the problems that you are facing. You will become aware of it when you begin to relax and can recall your dreams once more.
9. As you begin to recall and interpret more of your dreams you begin to realize that you have slowly discovered an amazing new world. Each dream will be like a mystery waiting to be understood. It could contain all the

suspense, thrills, twists and turns, ups and downs that mysteries entail. It could take you into a dim past or into a distant future. You are soon caught up with the wonder, exhilaration, fascination, and excitement which each dream provides. Every dream helps your personal growth and urges you to greater wholeness.

Recording Your Dreams

For the first few months, as you enter this new world, it may be useful to record your dreams. At my dream workshops, I often record every dream on audiotape. It is important to record the dream as told for the first time. The participants at my workshop are instructed not to discuss their dreams with anyone till they have shared it with the group. This is because the first narration is critical. A dreamer could be easily influenced by verbal and nonverbal reactions of others to his dream. He might unconsciously change the narrative based on these reactions. Additional important factors that require attention are the tone of voice, pauses, hesitations, coughs, facial expressions, and so on which are all clues to help its interpretation. The dreamers are rarely asked to narrate the dream again. Usually, when a person hears his dream being played back, he might want to change a statement, or some new facts or events may be remembered. According to Freud, what the dreamer had forgotten in his first narrative is also usually critical. If you prefer to write down your dreams, then a dream journal would be useful.

Your Dream Journal

Here are some guidelines to keep a Dream Journal:

- Write on only one side of the page, reserving the other side for notes and illustrations. For example, if you were in a strange castle with seven domes, you might like to illustrate it.
- Figures and forms which you cannot describe in words can be represented through illustrations. If you are an expressive person, you might like to illustrate your feelings. For example, a smiling face or an angry face.
- Put the date on the top right hand of the page. If you are not sure which side of midnight you have had the dream, then the date should indicate both the days. For example, 19/20 November 2003.
- If you are sure of the time of the dream, put it down under the date.
- Give a suitable title to your dream. It not only helps you to recall and identify it, but also carries your very own personal stamp. It is like a bit of creative writing, very similar to the title of a chapter of an ongoing novel. It might also inspire you to write your dreams in a creative way. It also adds a certain

mystery to your effort because you do not know what is coming next.

- Remember to write down the dream as early as possible in the morning. As the day wears out, so do the memories, especially the feelings associated with the dream. Write down everything you recall, including colours, odd shapes, sounds and conversations, however absurd they may be. The unconscious is unbelievably miserly. It does not waste any space. Everything in the dream is important and has meaning. Be honest with yourself. Do not censor, paraphrase or try to interpret or explain away what you experienced till you have recorded all of it.
- Start from the beginning. You might need to close your eyes for a few minutes and remember feelings in the dream, in order to be able to narrate it with emotion, rather than in a distant and intellectual manner. Write the dream in an easy and simple style, as if you are narrating it to your friends.
- The end of the dream is often very important, because it could contain the message of the dream summed up in a sentence. For example, as the dream ends you may see a hoarding or a banner by a roadside saying, 'Watch out!' or 'Take care'. Or you may see a gravestone with a message inscribed on it. Sometimes people see their guru

in the dream, who provides guidance or gives them advice like, 'Do not accept the new job offer.' All these are ways in which your unconscious is trying to communicate to you. So it is important to pay close attention to how the dream ends.

Spontaneous Recall

Often, people recall their dreams spontaneously, without any effort. The major factor in the spontaneous recall of dreams appears to be that you may have woken up directly from a dream by chance during the course of the night, or become aware that you are dreaming just prior to waking up in the morning. Hence, there is a greater possibility of remembering long, vivid, emotionally intense dreams, rather than short, vague and uninteresting ones. It seems that a sudden awakening from sleep normally results in more recall than gradual awakening. People with vivid imaginations are likely to produce more dramatic dreams than others. Experience has indicated that people who meditate have more clear and vivid dreams than others. Sometimes, you may not recall a dream on waking, but you may see someone or hear something during the course of the day, that will trigger off the memory of the dream, often in its entirety.

3

Seven Methods to Interpret Your Dreams

We are now at the most fascinating point in our journey. We have reached a strange and enchanting land where no maps exist. At this point we say goodbye to the old and popular notions about dreams, and get ready to move into a new world, equipped with a new language. The language of dreams. This new world, the dream state, is an independent state in consciousness. It has its own reality. In the East, dreams are seen as tools of transformation. They open invisible doors to subtler levels of physical, psychological and spiritual growth.

This chapter contains seven methods of dream interpretation. All seven are tried and tested methods. Some of them are relatively simple and easy to use. Others would require some practice and experience. The important common factor in all these methods is the underlying assumption that the only expert in dream interpretation is the dreamer himself. The assumption is based on the fact that only the dreamer knows what is really going on in his life and can see its connection with his dream. You will, in due course, learn several methods of interpreting dreams, and may even master some of them. But it would help, in the long run, to perceive yourself as facilitating the process, rather than providing answers.

Some Preliminaries

New values have emerged in dreamwork. We have moved away from the old psychoanalytic approach, in the process demystifying dream interpretation. The concept of 'client-centred therapy', espoused by Carl Rogers (1961), has influenced many dream psychologists.

On the very first day of my dream workshops, I make it a point to tell the participants, 'You should feel privileged that the dreamer is trusting you with the keys to his private world. You should tread softly, for you are entering a sacred space, the inner temple of a fellow human being.'

It is important for you to learn to be sensitive to others before you begin to interpret their dreams. You have to learn to listen with understanding, to feel and show empathy (not sympathy), and to suspend judgment. These are tough prerequisites to becoming an effective dream worker.

Unfortunately, most people are ill-prepared to work with dreams. Perhaps it is the stress and competitiveness of urban life that has made people insensitive. They rush to judgment, even before the dreamer has completed narrating his dream. The inept dream interpreter then tries to foist his own ideas on to the dreamer. I recall a humorous warning, 'Don't let Freud's sexual problems become your nightmares!'

In dreamwork, the dream must be interpreted with an open mind. The approach must be to listen with patience and focused attention, with great empathy—placing yourself in the shoes of the dreamer. Make the dream your own, yet be aware of your projections. It is truly amazing to experience the quality of silence in a dream group. Even the slightest sound is magnified several times. Many of us work with closed eyes so that our other senses are heightened. You have to learn to listen to what the dreamer says (the content of his dream), what he does not say (his non-verbal cues—body language, tone of voice) and what he cannot say without your help (he is inhibited, or inarticulate). In working with dreams, therefore, you have to develop a soft, gentle approach.

Meet Monte Ullman

There are probably less than a dozen people in the world who know everything that there is to be known about the psychology of dreams and dreaming. Montague (Monte) Ullman (1970) is one of them. He speaks with an authority that few can match. So it will be appropriate to begin our foray into dream interpretation with a method that is largely based on his work, but which has been adapted to local culture and conditions.

Method I: Using Feelings and Metaphors

This method is very effective when used in a group, but it can be used individually as well.

This is the step-by-step method used in a group:

Step 1. I begin by asking the dreamer to take, what we lightheartedly call 'the hot seat'. Once seated, I ask him to relax, close his eyes and try and get in touch with the feelings in the dream. I remind him that everything in the dream is important, including shapes, sounds and colours. However bizarre and irrational the events may seem, he should share them with the group as if he were recounting a story to a group of friends, without paraphrasing, censoring or interpreting the dream.

Step 2. The group is allowed to ask the dreamer for any clarification of facts. They are warned not to probe or put the dreamer on the defensive. The questions must be neutral, like, 'Do you know what time of the day it was?' or 'How old were you in the dream?'

Step 3. At this stage, the group is asked to keep the dreamer out of the discussion. They should not even make eye contact. Each member of the group then speaks as though the dream is his own. He picks up the feelings in the dream. For example, someone in the group will start the process by saying, 'If it were my dream I would pick up feelings of sadness, anger, frustration ...' Other group members follow. The dreamer quietly listens to the large number of feelings that people pick up in one dream. Some seem relevant, others irrelevant, but they set him thinking. When everybody has completed this exercise, you move to the next step.

Step 4. The group looks for metaphors in the dream. What do all those objects and characters stand for? For example, someone in the group might say, 'If it were my dream, the witch would stand for my mother-in-law...' Or another might say, 'If it were my dream, the old car would stand for my body, which is suffering wear and tear...' The group will identify and suggest several possible metaphors, some relevant to the dreamer, others he will simply discard.

Step 5. The dream is handed back to the dreamer, who is thanked for allowing the group to play around with his dream. He is then asked whether there are any events occurring in his life that reflect the feelings and metaphors in the dream. Sure enough, while the group has been exchanging ideas on feelings and metaphors, the dreamer has obtained a clear insight into his dream. Sometimes, he is pleasantly surprised with the 'ah-ha' experience he gets. It means the interpretation is correct.

Following Step 5, the dreamer discusses the insights he has obtained and what the dream means. The group could also help him clarify some issues or help him resolve others. Even at this stage, the group must remember that the dream belongs to the person dreaming it, therefore he will always understand its meaning the most.

How to Use the Method: The Jungle Bungle

Here is the dream of a middle-aged manager from a large private sector company. He recounted the dream saying he had no idea what it could signify:

> I am in a jungle and I am behind a counter, something like a fast food counter, and I am on the servicing side and wearing a ten-gallon hat. There are two people sitting across the counter. I don't recall one of them, but the second person is Jimmy Carter (President, USA). And in the background, just a little behind him, I see three very rough - looking characters. One of them has Mongolian features, heavily armed with another person with a black patch on his eye. I don't recall his features at all. But all three were heavily armed and they were standing there laughing. And of course, it is a normal jungle with trees around and we are in a little opening.

Now make this your dream. The first step is to identify the

feelings, and to write them all down. My dream group identified: excitement and fear (from the jungle image), power and responsibility (from the ten-gallon hat), anxiety (VIP customers), fear of impending violence (from the three ruffians) and hope (from the little opening).

Next you work on the metaphors. What could these images possibly stand for? Here is what the group came up with:

Jungle: Organizational jungle
Fast food counter: Marketing activity
I am...servicing side: Marketing manager
Ten-Gallon hat: Senior position, heavy responsibility
Jimmy Carter, etc.: Very important customers, VIPs
Three armed characters: Competitors, union leaders, colleagues, subordinates
In a little opening: The possibility of getting out of this situation, to escape

Interpretation

The dreamer is a senior manager in a large company. He is a marketing manager, who is extremely efficient and serves important customers. He is now facing a big problem, from competitors or colleagues or union leaders. But the dream is telling him not to worry, there is a way out and he can easily find it.

The dreamer was in fact, a senior marketing manager working in a very competitive environment. Though he was in a powerful position in the company, he perceived three new entrants as posing a threat to him because one of them was related to the chairman of the company. Just before going to bed, he had worked out a plan to deal with his opponents. The dream had reinforced his plan and given him the green signal to go ahead.

How to Use the Method with Your Own Dreams

To use Method I for interpreting your own dreams, you will have to begin by writing down your dream in full on the right-hand page of your journal, leaving the left-hand page empty to be used for illustrations, comments, day-residue and pre-sleep thoughts. Underline the images in the dream which evoke feelings in you. Circle the images which stand for metaphors. Use separate colours, if possible. On the opposite page, write down the feelings and the metaphors. Draw them where words fail you. Look at the day-residue and your pre-sleep thoughts. What is going on in your life at the moment that matches the emotions and metaphors in the dream? How do recent events relate to the feelings, thoughts and images in the dream? The dream may be simply mundane, a 'house-keeping dream', clearing up the mind of cluttered thoughts. More likely, it is working on a problem that you are facing or are not willing to confront. In that case, the dream may provide clarification of the problem, alternative suggestions for its solution, or a clear and unambiguous solution. Often, the end of the dream has a message for you or, perhaps, the solution itself. When working on your dream, always ask yourself, 'What is the message of the dream?'

Method II: Following the Dream Ego

A simple method to interpret your dream is to follow the dream ego. As you examine your dream, ask yourself, 'What am I doing in my dream?' You may be taking part in a competition, receiving a prize, debating in school or simply running, falling or flying. The dreamer in the dream is called the dream ego. By watching the dream ego you obtain a great deal of information about the dreamer's waking life. People dream that they rush to the station and just miss a train—and you will find that they may have just missed an opportunity. Or, you may be able to pick up a clear pattern of behaviour that you have adopted since childhood. The dream ego method works best with long dreams, where the dreamer is unusually active. Often, such dreams may cover a long period of the dreamer's life. The following instance chronicles the dream of a middle-aged woman called Asha, who was facing a crisis in her life:

The Doberman Who Split

I had gone somewhere. It is rather in the wilderness. After finishing my work, I go to my father and ask him to take me back home. He starts driving to go home by a new road, and I tell him, 'Let's go by the road which we came from', but he insists on going through a gate which is just in front of him, and as he approaches it, he realizes he can't get through. There's a bump in between. So just at the last minute, he turns to his right. That road is very rough and the car develops some problem. Some part of the car is rolling off the body. I get off, I pick the part up, put it straight and help him push the car backwards. There is a young girl who comes and helps also. My father smiles at her. Just as she came from nowhere, she disappears. The car is being repaired by my father where I am not required. Just behind, I see a market where beetroot is being sold, so I think I'll put it in my henna and apply it on my hair. I don't buy anything. I think, may be, there are other markets ahead and I'll go and see. I go rather far and I want to come back. I think to myself 'I'll use the same road which I came by, so that I don't get lost.' I can't contact my father and can't find where both of us should be waiting for each other. As I walk, I realize that I am still lost and I come to the house of somebody whom I know. There is a

Doberman there. I enter the building and I irritate this dog a little in a playful way. He gets angry, and I'm thinking to myself, 'He has a split personality, one good and one bad.' And the dog actually splits into two dogs! The bad one attacks me but I am carrying a metal kind of rusted bag which I put in his mouth to prevent myself from being injured. I slide my hand off this bag and now the dog is holding the bag so he doesn't realize I've taken my hand off. The good dog is standing looking down helplessly without doing anything. And now I'm stuck. I don't know what I should do. I'm afraid to move towards the gate which is just two feet away from me. So the dream ends with me standing in an uncertain state.

How to Work on this Dream

Read the dream carefully. Ask yourself: 'What is the dreamer doing in her dream?' The answer would be:

1. She finds herself in the wilderness.
2. She wants her father to take her home by the same road by which they had travelled earlier.
3. Against her wishes, he takes a new road.
4. As a result, they hit a bump and the car breaks down.
5. She does not help in repairing the car, but leaves him to complete the job.

6. She watches a little girl appear and disappear.
7. She is lost and separated from her father (husband?).
8. She encounters a Doberman which she irritates.
9. The dog splits. The bad part attacks her. The good part is helpless.
10. She temporarily saves herself by shoving her bag in the dog's mouth.
11. She is two feet away from freedom (the gate) but finds herself stuck. She does not know what to do.

Now ask the dreamer, 'What is going on in your life that resembles these actions? Do the feelings and metaphors convey something to you?'

When Asha worked on her dream, this is what emerged:

The setting in the dream itself is significant. At this point in her life, she finds herself 'in the wilderness'. Her marriage is a wreck and she plans to 'go home'. The father in the dream later becomes her husband, who has differences with her from the outset and never heeds her advice. The dream covers the entire period of her life from the time of her marriage. At the time of her dream, she was in a dilemma whether to divorce her husband or not. The broken-down car indicates her broken marriage and the young girl who suddenly appears is her only daughter. Now that the marriage is broken, she has to fend for herself and goes in search of a livelihood. She is lost for a while but decides to use old skills to earn a living. The

Doberman represents her husband who has good and attractive qualities that endear him to the dreamer but also bad ones that scare her and make him unbearable. At the time of the dream, the husband lived separately from her. She was now free to 'walk out of the gate', just two feet away, to her freedom. However, she was 'stuck', unable to decide on divorce. After working on the dream, she understood what was going on in her life and why it was important to move away from her husband. The dream helped her to make the decision to be free.

Strephon Kaplan-Williams (1986) suggests steps we might take to use this method. They have been adapted to make them easier for you to understand.

1. Starting from the beginning of the dream, describe literally what the dream ego is or is not doing.
2. Describe what the dream ego is or is not feeling. Doing is action. Feeling is being.

   Choose certain key descriptions and re-describe them in generalized terms. Thus, 'My dream ego is afraid to move towards the gate which is just two feet away from me,' might become 'The dream ego is unable to take the action needed to be free.'
3. List possible underlying attitudes which may be governing the dream ego's actions or feelings. Thus, from the dream with the Doberman adversary, we might

obtain these possibilities for attitudes. 'Good and attractive qualities that endure him to the dreamer.' 'When I am attacked, I am able to take action to save myself.' 'I have the strength to deal with certain negative forces.'

4. Choose those attitudes that are positive, valuable, and life-affirming for you, and those that are negative. The context for this evaluation may be the goals in the dream itself, or other goals or values for you. For instance, in the above example from an actual dream, when the car (marriage) breaks down, the dream ego goes out on her own to search for a living. The negative part is being stuck when faced with a dilemma. On the other hand, moving away from the Doberman was effective. Thus, there must be some other way that can be found to cope with the situation.
5. Choose those negative attitudes which seem most appropriate and change them by affirming them. To create an affirmation, take a negative attitude and re-write it as a life-affirming, reality-affirming statement. For example, the attitude 'It is better to avoid painful decisions than to face them,' can be changed to 'It is better to face up to the threat and escape from a dangerous situation.'

Then, using your journal, write this statement down several

times on one side of the page and write whatever comes to mind on the other. This will usually be the 'negative mass' evoked by the new attitude. You are re-training yourself in new attitudes, which are now real values and which are more integrative and life affirming. Keep making the affirmation until it wins over the negative mass. Or, write a new affirmation which includes the new and the negative attitudes evoked together, if this will make your affirmation more realistic.

For example, the statement 'It is better to avoid painful decisions than to face them' becomes as an affirmation 'I am more able to directly face the threats in my life.' If the voice of the 'negative mass' strongly says, 'No, you are not,' then re-write the affirmation as 'I am more able to face directly some of the threats in my life.'

A Sea of Troubles

Often, the technique of following the dream ego makes the meaning quickly obvious and clear. A good example would be the following dream of a brilliant scientist who worked for a public sector research & development (R&D) unit:

> I don't know if it's day or night. I am walking and it is completely dark due to the heavy clouds overhead. Suddenly it starts raining, followed by lightning and

> thunder. I want to go back but decide against it. So, I continue walking and take a shortcut. I find there is a big hill that comes in the way. I decide to climb the hill. As I start climbing, halfway up the hill a cliff appears from nowhere, creating a new hurdle. I am not able to climb the cliff. Then I see a lot of snakes around me. I want to get rid of the snakes. I see a tree and jump up and get hold of a branch. All of a sudden the snakes disappear and I jump back to the ground.

Using the 'Follow the Dream Ego' method, the dreamer could easily match the feelings and metaphors in the dream with the current events in his life.

As a well-known scientist, he had been invited to present a paper at an important scientific conference in the United States. Due to the envy and politics within his corporation, and the insensitive bureaucracy of the government, he faced endless and unexpected hurdles throughout. He believed that the hill and cliffs and the inclement weather represented problems with the government and the environment, while the snakes were his own colleagues. He saw the tree as his CEO, who intervened to ensure that the way was cleared for him to attend the conference.

Dream Ego and Problems of Identity

The most common symbol in our dreams is the dream ego, the

image of ourselves in the dream. By watching the dream ego, we can see the kind of identity we have, or sometimes our problems with this identity, as the following dream of a research scientist shows: 'I am working in a laboratory where I don't know whether I am teaching or working as a coolie ...'

Dealing with the conflict in identity is an important function of dreams, and the dream ego technique helps to resolve the conflict. This method reveals how we operate in dreams and in waking life and helps us to discover the unconscious attitudes, values and beliefs that govern our behaviour. We begin to notice that the behaviour of the dream ego is often similar to our waking behaviour. Working on this difference to ensure congruence also ensures authentic behaviour. The dream ego often portrays the dreamer behaving in new and creative ways in the dream, indicating that the dreamer can risk trying out new behaviour in his waking life as well, with positive consequences. A very important aspect of dream ego work is that the dreamer can perceive a wide range of emotions which he does not express in the waking state. He should try and re-experience these emotions and treat the dream as a rehearsal for re-enacting many aspects of his life.

Method III: Gayle's Interview Technique

Gayle Delaney (1979), a renowned dream psychologist in the

United States and Europe, has done pioneering work that has greatly enhanced our understanding of dreams. Gayle's 'dream interview' method takes the interpretation of dreams out of the hands of experts and empowers the best interpreters of all—the dreamers themselves! Her breakthrough techniques help dreamers to quickly and simply interpret their dreams to resolve challenges and problems, both at the personal and organizational level.

The Interviewer's Tools

The basic tool you will need in order to use this technique is an inquisitive style. You will need to know what the most relevant questions to ask the dreamer are. You will also need to gain experience in asking appropriate questions that follow up on the dreamer's responses, or lack of them. You will have to develop an appreciation for dream puns and metaphors, along with a sense of creative play in piecing together the dream puzzle. While Carl Rogers (1961) did not work with dreams, his client-centred approach in counselling and therapy is a good value system to adopt. You must also have the ability to re-experience the emotions of the dream. It is through re-living the way we felt at different points in a dream, that we are led to recognize areas in our present lives that give rise to similar feelings.

The best way to learn how to use the Interview Method

to interpret dreams is to actually work on one. Here is the dream of a scientist working in a large R&D centre:

Shattered Glass and Dreams

> The setting is our R&D Centre. I am very upset and I am sitting at my table at my work place. One of my colleagues, Dr Prasad, comes and tells me about the latest work he has done, about his articles that have been published in the latest publications. I can remember the name of the journal where his paper has been accepted. It is the Bulletin of Chemical Study of Japan. I don't remember the others. I think there were three publications. Dr Ramadorai, a senior colleague comes in and I request that we be given a proper place to sit and work, not the way we are working at present. I remember that there is a lot of dust around. I sprinkle some water and the dust settles. I meet another colleague who tries to console me. I have a glass tumbler in my hand. I am looking at it when suddenly I find myself in my village, in a corner of a street. After that corner, there are endless fields of paddy. I remember that I have spent many years in this place and I realize that I have not grown. I get so upset and disturbed that I smash the glass on the ground in anger. After some time the people living in the house come out and I realize that I should remove all those glass pieces, so that it does not hurt them. I start removing those glass pieces. After that I can't remember anything.

Dream Interviewer's Cue Card

Let us now use the dream interview technique to interpret this dream. The cue card is used to ask questions to which the dreamer replies. This is how it works:

When you re-experience the feelings you had in the dream, do they remind you of anything in your current life?

Yes. It seems to be about my work.

Describe the opening setting of the dream: place, mood and feelings. How does it feel to be in this setting? Or, what does it feel like, or how do you feel as you stand there?

It is my workplace. Right now I feel rather disturbed. I am not happy going to work. I feel very troubled.

Does this remind you of anything? Does the location, the mood, or do these feelings remind you of a situation in your life?

Yes, it reminds me of the conflict I am facing at my workplace.

Who is Dr Prasad?

He is my colleague, a fellow scientist. We joined the R&D Centre together.

What is Dr Prasad like?

He is a competent scientist. He knows how to get along with the bosses.

What is Dr Prasad like in your dream? What is he doing in your dream?

He is behaving as usual. He is boasting about his achievements. He makes me feel small and inadequate.

What is your waking relationship with Dr Prasad like?

On the surface we are friends and colleagues. In reality he is very competitive and political.

Does Dr Prasad remind you of anything or anyone in your life?

He appears in the dream as himself. There are no other scientists who boast and act like him. He is not very popular.

Is there some part of you that is like Dr Prasad? If you were a psychologist, what would you say were the reasons that Dr Prasad turned out this way?

We are both keen on research, equally qualified, but he does not work as hard as I do. I am told that even though both of us were selected together by the Centre, he used influence to get in. His problem is that he is too ambitious and wants to make his mark in a hurry.

What is the 'dust around' indicate in your dream? What is it like?

I think it indicates the callousness of the top management

regarding the scientists working in the R&D Centre. There is no thought given either to the technical facilities or the administrative support. But most important we have no plan for our professional and career development. We are stuck in the same position for years. Our seniors are powerless, and can't do anything about the situation.

Does the 'dust around' in your dream remind you of anything, any part of yourself, or anyone in your life? How?

Yes, it tells me I am in a chaotic place where I have no future.

So, you are sitting in your office quite upset. Dr Prasad comes in and tells you about his latest publications in which you don't seem interested. You find that the workplace is in a mess and dirty and you try to clean it unsuccessfully. Then you speak to your seniors about the situation and discover that they are in a similar situation and quite powerless to do anything about it. You are disturbed and a friend tries to console you. Then you find yourself in your native village where you angrily break a glass which was in your hand. Then quickly try and pick up the pieces. Is there something I have missed?

No.

Now, how do you understand the dream?

I think it reflects my present state of mind and what is

happening at my workplace. I think I go to my village, where I spent several years, and was very secure and happy, to find a safe place to express my anger and frustration. Having done so, I immediately realize in our organization that it would be dangerous and dysfunctional to express my anger too strongly. So, I probably feel guilty and am 'picking up the pieces'. Thank you, that was very helpful. The dream makes sense. I was wondering what it was all about.

Method IV: The Martian Technique

This method is very effective when you encounter strange objects or persons in a dream. It is almost a short cut to get to the very heart of the dream, that is, to its core meaning. Gayle Delaney uses it as part of her dream interviewing approach. The method entails pretending that you are from another planet and asking the dreamer to explain what ordinary objects mean to an alien. Thus, in his effort to explain these objects to an alien, the dreamer gives away clues on what they actually stand for. You can start by saying to the dreamer, 'I come from Mars and I don't know a thing about earth life. Could you explain this "cow" in your dream, so that a Martian can understand it? What is a cow?' In responding to you, the dreamer will actually give you clues on what the cow symbolizes in his dream.

Given below is an actual example of this method, in order to understand its effectiveness.

There was a class of young executives who were at a Management Training Centre in Pune, undergoing a four-week course. At the end of the session one evening, the group planned a visit to the Katraj Snake Park. However, one of them named Anil, was so afraid of snakes that he refused to go. When he was asked the reason for his fear, Anil was not very forthcoming with the story, saying 'It has a long history.' Nevertheless, he was persuaded to tell the group the following story:

The Smiling Snake

> As you know, I am a manager in a steel company. For many years, even before starting to work, I have had a very disturbing recurring dream. I see myself running along a country road wearing pink boxing gloves, vest and shorts. I keep on running and then suddenly stop. I look down and see a green snake move in the grass. The snake raises its hood and smiles. I turn around and run back to my house. I sit outside the house in a garden chair and I am drinking a cup of tea. Suddenly, I hear some rustling in the grass near me. A snake pops its head up and smiles. I am upset. I get up, put my hands out and try to shoo the snake away. I keep saying 'shoo, shoo, shoo…' till I wake up and find that I am standing on top of the dining

room table with my hands out still saying, 'shoo, shoo, shoo...'

Often, I make so much noise that my family wakes up and comes into the dining room. We have tried everything-doctors, astrologers, vastu shastra experts. I have even changed my bedroom. The bed was moved to different angles but nothing seems to work. The dream recurs.'

When Anil had completed his narration of the dream, I helped him to interpret it in the following manner:

Author: Do those boxing gloves remind you of anything?

Anil: Yes, of my boarding school days.

Author: Would you like to tell us more about it?

Anil: Well... Actually it was terrible. Every time I went into the ring I got hammered. But my boxing coach kept insisting that I was good, my technique was excellent. I had to persist with the game. Evening after evening I went in. And evening after evening I got beaten. And my coach just sat in the front row, below the ring, and kept urging me to fight. One day, a small Nepali boy was my opponent and I thought to myself, 'Finally, I have got my chance.' Unfortunately, I underrated the little fellow. He thrashed me. I was so humiliated, I came back to the dressing room and hung up my gloves forever.

Author: Good. Anil, if I was a Martian, somebody from another planet. How would you explain what that smiling snake is to me? We do not have such creatures in Mars.

Anil: It is a dangerous creature. It is slithery and slippery. It is not easily visible when it camouflages itself. Its bite is fatal. This snake is smiling, so it is hiding something. I feel very scared of its friendliness.

Author: What I would like you to do, is to get up on the table, close your eyes, and try and get in touch with the feelings in the dream. Keep your eyes closed. Just try and recall the dream. Get in touch with the feelings. Take a few deep breaths. That's right. Try and remember what you told the Martian about the snake. Does that description remind you of someone? When it seems natural, put your hands out and begin to shoo away the snake. Shoo, shoo, shoo. Louder. Move your palms more vigorously. Right... is there an image that you see?

Anil (breathing heavily and in an angry outburst): Yes, it's my bloody boxing coach. He is the snake in the grass. He is the snake in the grass! He was really a son of a bitch. I have got it. (He hits his right fist into his left palm.)

Author: Right. Anil now come down carefully and share with us what's going on in your mind.

Anil: Yes, my coach was a snake in the grass. All the time he was smiling and pretending to encourage me, but each time I was humiliated. And he could see it. Again and again, I pleaded with him that boxing was not my game. But he insisted, and being a boarding school, I had no option but to go along. I hate him. He was really the cause of a lot of my misery. (Anil puts his head down and sobs.)

Needless to say, that evening Anil went to the snake park and saw the reptiles without any fear. His recurrent dream disappeared.

Method V: Bringing the Dream to Resolution

This is a method that you will find easy to use. It should be used when the dream has ended at a tantalizing point, leaving the dreamer in animated suspension. Sometimes, you find that you have been able to interpret most of the dream but you are left with a feeling of incompletion. You feel the dream needs closure, a natural ending. You feel you have missed the message of the dream. This situation often occurs in a group. If the dreamer becomes emotional, his fellow group members may feel uncomfortable and end the session early. Group members try to console a dreamer who may be grieving, and in the process there is no closure of the dream. The dreamer is left feeling incomplete. That is when this method works best. It helps to understand the dream and triggers transformation.

Learning to Let Go

Without resolution, the entire being of the incomplete dream hangs on, preventing new life from being given birth. An old habit, dysfunctional behaviour, or a chronic symptom, will not just fade away. Something has to die when its time has come to make place for the new. This is what dream resolution does. People go through life carrying the burden of old hurts and sorrows long after the event has faded into the past. Sometimes, out of compassion (as in the following dream), the unconscious literally takes you to the graveyard to make it easy for you to bury the past. However, as you might guess, it is not easy. Thus, one can understand why the young man who dreamt about his struggle to get rid of an old and dysfunctional pattern of behaviour, was afraid to take the final step:

The Gravedigger Laughs

> There are two freshly dug empty graves and two grave stones. Someone is chiselling some words into the stones. The writing is between the lines already written. The words are, '...then you will be dead'. My dog and I lie in the graves, thinking that the answer to the riddle may be found there. The person chiselling the stone drops the stones on us, trying to trap us in the graves. We leap out in time. The gravedigger laughs and says, 'Did you get it? Then you will really be dead!'

The dream could not be more explicit. However, perhaps the dreamer is not yet ready to die, or to let go of his old behaviour to change. Death is essential for transformation and change to take place. We have become so used to the old self, to the old habit, to the old aspect of a certain behaviour pattern, that we confuse the death of that part of the ego with one's own physical death. We would rather cling to old habits, which make us feel secure, than risk changing our ways, thus opening the door to the unknown.

Kaplan-Williams (1986) describes the transformation cycle as follows:

+ Things exist in an original unity, all merged into one harmonious whole.
+ The differentiation of opposites begins to occur via conflicts developing between the various parts.
+ An imbalance occurs in which certain opposites are exalted or given much of the available energy. This evokes compensation, or the tendency to rebalance opposites with equal amounts of energy.
+ An enantiodromic cycle is set in motion, in which energy keeps flowing from one side to another in a see-saw manner.
+ The danger exists of going into one extreme and fixating there as a way of solving the conflict.

- If this danger is resisted by the ego, and a balanced tension is maintained between the opposites, then transformation can occur.
- Maintaining the tension between the opposites allows a unity to develop between them which brings resolution to the conflict.
- A new harmony exists which has both unity and the differentiation of opposites.
  This is the transformation of old into new.

Three Practical Ways to Bring Resolution

Practical ways of bringing resolution to an unresolved dream involves carrying the dream forward in the waking state. In the dream images there is an inherent evolving potential. You may:

1. Sleep again and try to continue the dream;
2. Re-enter the dream in a meditative state; or,
3. Simply use a pen and paper to carry the dream forward. It is as if you are a script writer for a television serial and are planning the next episode. The difference is crucial, as while the television script writer has the audience in mind, the dreamer has to go deep within himself to allow the truth to emerge. It is possible to continue the dream in writing without interfering with it. You must let your pen just flow, without letting your mind interfere. This

will seem difficult at first, but as you continue writing, it will feel seamless.

The Gravedigger Laughs

To illustrate the technique, the dreamer of the Graveyard dream narrated earlier was asked to use his imagination to write down what could have possibly happened next, until he brought the dream to resolution. Given below is what he wrote:

> I am anxious, a bit fearful as to what the gravedigger is saying. His manic laughter has completely put me on my defensive. He looks so self-assured compared to me. In my dream, I think, 'How can I solve my riddle if I am dead?' I fail to understand this statement and the riddle mystifies me further. But, surprisingly my dog is very calm. On one side I am fearful of the gravedigger but at the same time I have a feeling that the answers to all my questions lie with him. I am intimidated by the gravedigger but I do not want to show him. I look around to see if there is anybody there. There is darkness around me. Only my dog is sitting by my side faithfully. Again I look closely at the letters chiselled on the gravestone popping out at me. So, I calmly ask him, 'What do you mean that I will get it?'

At that moment the gravedigger suddenly gives me a benign smile which reminds me of someone I love a lot. All my fears and anxieties leave me and I feel a strong pull towards this man. As he continues to look at me serenely, I get an insight into the statement. Yes! I have to die. I have to die. My old pattern of behaviour needs to die. Now I understand the true meaning of this death. It is not my physical death that the gravedigger is talking about but the death of my old self, my old habit and the old aspect to my certain behaviour. As I get this insight, I gratefully look around for the gravedigger but suddenly I find myself alone. There are no graves, no gravestones, no inscriptions on the grave and even my faithful dog is not around. And the gravedigger? He has just vanished in thin air. But, the surprising part of the whole event is that I am alone but not feeling lonely. I am feeling calm and collected. There is a new exhilaration within. A new spring in my footsteps. I feel completely rejuvenated. As if the canvas of my life has taken new colours. Fresh colours, which give me fresh hope and faith in myself. Now, I can see my old dysfunctional pattern clearly and unemotionally. As I get more and more aware of it, there is a sense of release within me... A new sense of freedom.

This is how the dreamer could have successfully brought resolution to the dream.

Method VI: Gestalt Dreamwork

The word gestalt is of German origin, and has been defined as an integrated whole, something not simply the sum of its elements. Fritz Perls, the founder of gestalt therapy, believed that dreams urged us to greater wholeness. He viewed the human being as an organic whole. A person, like anything else in nature, is meant to grow, fructify and die. However, with the dubious gift of the mind, he prevents his own growth. Thus, he projects the parts of himself that he does not like and does not wish to own, on to others. For example, if he feels guilty about his anger, he will project it on the other person. Rather than own his anger, and say to himself, 'I am angry' he will say, 'You are angry with me.' Often, when a child asks his father, 'Why are you angry?' the father will deny it, shouting angrily, 'I am not angry!' The whole world can see his anger, but he cannot. He is unaware and unwilling to own his feelings, so he projects it on to others. Therefore it is always someone else who is angry, envious, callous or afraid.

Similarly, Fritz Perls believed that people also project those parts of themselves that they do not wish to own into their dreams. His approach to dream interpretation is by saying to the dreamer, 'Every person in the dream, every object in the dream, is you. So, the entire effort in dreamwork is to help you to re-own these parts of yourself that you have disowned.'

To interpret a dream, Fritz Perls introduced a role-playing arrangement. He encouraged the dreamer to enter into a dialogue with every element of the dream, animate or inanimate. Perls considered each such element as signifying some unfinished emotional business left over from the past. He referred to them as 'emotional holes'.

Mother Beulah's Doormat

Let me give you an example: Mother Beulah, the German Superior of a Catholic convent had the following dream:

> In my dream, I see a small, well-built white cottage in a suburban area. It has a sturdy wooden door. The entrance to the cottage is a white wicket gate which is not locked. There is a doormat at the entrance of the cottage. That is all I can remember.

The gestalt approach of Fritz Perls was used to interpret the dream. In this approach, the dreamer is asked to retell the dream from the point of view of the various objects or people in the dream. In Mother Beulah's dream, there were no people, so she was first asked to relate the dream from the point of view of the cottage. She began by saying, 'I am the cottage in Beulah's dream. I am small, sturdy, dependable in all weathers, warm and comforting.'

Next she was asked to relate the dream from the point of view of the wicket gate in the dream. She said, 'I am the gate in Beulah's dream. I am white and fragile. There is no lock on me. So, people come in and go as they wish. I feel vulnerable and exposed.' Then she was asked to tell the dream from the viewpoint of the doormat. She started, 'I am the doormat in Beulah's dream. Yes, I am just a doormat…' and then broke down, first weeping softly, then sobbing loudly, finally going into a catharsis. Through her angry tears, she said:

'Yes, I am only a doormat. Just a bloody doormat. Nobody cares. They just trample on me, leave their dirt on me, never bothering to even say thank you. It's true, Sisters come and cry on my shoulder but on whose shoulder should I cry? I am also a woman. I have also feelings but I am simply taken for granted. I am not blaming anyone but the Sisters use my skin colour as an excuse to distance themselves from me and leave me alone. I feel so lonely. I am so lonely…'

When she was through with her weeping, the energy changed in her body. Her face looked different, almost radiant. The nuns who had accompanied her could not believe what they had witnessed. They showed regret for being unaware of Mother Beulah's needs. They expressed their love and gratitude to her for sharing her innermost self with them.

Through the Gestalt approach to dream interpretation, Beulah was able to recognize and own parts of herself that she had disowned and had projected into her dream. The method used made her feel complete and more peaceful within herself. By expressing regret and gratitude to her, the nuns helped her dream to fully understand her.

The Doctrine according to Perls

Fritz Perls (1996) says:

> 'I believe that every part of the dream is a part of yourself—not just the person, but every item, every mood, anything that comes across. My favourite example is: A patient dreams he is leaving my office and goes to Central Park. And he goes across the bridle path (where horses and dogs are walked), into the Park. So I ask him, "Now play the bridle path." He answers indignantly, "What? And let everybody shit and crap on me?" You see, he really got the identification. I let the patient play all these parts, because only by really playing can you get the full identification, and the identification is the counteraction to the alienation. Alienation means "That's not me, that's something else, something strange, something not belonging to me." And often you encounter quite a bit of resistance against

playing this alienated part. You don't want to re-own, take back, those parts of yourself which you have pushed out of your personality. This is the way you have improved yourself. This is the advantage of role-playing, and if I let the patient do all the roles himself, we get a clearer picture. If you do everything yourself, then we know we are within ourself.'

Saying Goodbye in Gestalt

Many people have been unable to say goodbye and close a relationship that terminated in death, divorce or separation. Very often, people hold on to 'dead' relationships because there is a great deal of unfinished business between the two people before the relationship suddenly ended.

Some people appear so lifeless when they are recounting the dream, that you have a feeling they have identified with the dead person. In such situations, this is a useful though difficult technique to use and requires both experience and training in gestalt therapy.

The first step is to ask the dreamer whether he would like to talk about his relationship with the dead person (or about the dead relationship). Generally, after some initial hesitation, the person begins to talk, and with a little bit of gentle urging, explores the residual feelings if any, that he has about the relationship. At this point, the dreamer is asked whether he would like to say goodbye to the dead person. If he volunteers to do so, the stage is set for a dialogue with the dead person by placing an empty chair in front of the dreamer. This is called 'The Empty Chair Technique.'

He is then asked to imagine the dead person, in this case, his mother, sitting in the chair opposite him. For instance, what does he experience, seeing her there? He is encouraged to talk directly to her, to tell her all the experiences he has had with her that he treasures, that he is grateful for, that have helped him carry on with life. He must remember that he is trying to complete unfinished business, thus not to leave any things unsaid. He is also encouraged to tell her the things that he resented about her but was unable to express directly while she was alive.

The dreamer starts softly and slowly, but with a little urging, becomes completely involved in the process. In almost every case, there is a great deal of emotion that is expressed—grief, love, hurt and anger. When the dreamer seems to have no more unfinished business or is emotionally exhausted, he is asked to say 'Goodbye' and to finally let go. It is a cathartic process. The results of this method are amazing. People report that they are able to drop the negative thoughts about the dead person out of their minds. They also begin to feel lighter, more energetic and have an increased interest in life and other people.

A Clinical Example

Stephen Tobin, who pioneered this method, gives a clinical example of his work:

'The following is a re-creation of some work I did with a woman with whom I had had no previous contact, in a weekend workshop. The woman, whom I shall call "Mrs R," was a married housewife in her mid-thirties. She spoke in a very mechanical way, sounding like a child who was reciting a poem she had been forced to memorize but didn't understand. In her relationship with her husband and children she played the part of a masochistic martyr, controlling them by showing how much they made her "suffer". Our work on her saying goodbye to her dead mother started during a dream in which her mother appeared. While working on the dream, her voice and demeanor suddenly changed; she began to cry and sounded whiny and complaining. I asked her if she had some unfinished business with her mother.'

Mrs R: Well... if only she had loved me, things would be different. But she didn't and...and I've never had any real mother love (crying).

S: (Stephen Tobin): Put your mother in that chair and say that to her.

Mrs R: If only she had cared for me, I'd be much better today.

S: I want you to say this to her, not to me. Can you imagine her sitting there in front of you?

Mrs R: Yes, I see her as she looked when she was still alive. Mother, if you had only loved me. Why couldn't you ever tell me you loved me? Why did you always criticize me? (almost a wail, more tears).

S: Now switch over to the other chair and play your mother (she moves to the other chair and doesn't say anything).

S: What do you experience as your mother?

Mrs R: I-I-I don't know…I don't know what she would say.

S: Of course you don't know. She's not around any more. You're playing the part of you that is your mother. Just say whatever you experience there.

Mrs R: Oh, I see. Well, I don't know what to say to her.

S: Say that to her.

Mrs R M (Mrs R as Mother): I don't know what to say to you. I never knew what to say to you. I really did love you, you know that. Look at all the things I did for you, and you never appreciated it (voice sounds defensive and whiny).

S: Now switch back and reply as yourself.

Mrs RS (as Self): You never loved me! All you ever did was criticize me. Nothing I ever did was good enough! (voice beginning to sound more whiny). When I got married to J you disapproved, you were always coming over and telling me what I was doing wrong with the kids. Oh, you never came right out and said anything, but you were always making snide remarks or saying, 'Now, dear, wouldn't it be a good idea to put another blanket on the baby.' You made my life miserable; I was always worrying about you criticizing me. And now I'm having all this trouble with J. (breaks down and starts to cry).

S: Did you hear your voice?

Mrs. RS: Yes.

S: What did you hear in it?

Mrs RS: Well, I guess I sounded kind of complaining. Like I'm feeling sorry, like I'm feeling mad.

S: You sounded more like feeling self-pity. Try this on for size: say to your mother, 'Look what you've done to me. It's all your fault.'

Mrs. RS: Look what you've done. Everything's your fault.

S: Now let yourself switch back and forth as you find yourself changing roles.

Mrs RM: Come on, stop blaming me for everything. You are always complaining about something. If you had been better—if you had been a decent daughter, I wouldn't have had to criticize you so much.

Mrs RS: Oh, oh, (under her breath) damn. (She's swinging her right leg slightly).

S: Notice your leg.

Mrs RS: I-I'm shaking it.

S: Exaggerate that, shaking it harder.

Mrs RS: (Shakes leg harder, it begins to look like a kick).

S: Can you imagine doing that to your mother?

Mrs RS: No, but I-I-I'm sure feeling pissed at her.

S: Say this to her.

Mrs RS: I feel pissed off at you! I hate you!

S: Say that louder.

Mrs RS: I hate you! (Volume higher, but still some holding back).

S: Louder!

Mrs RS: I hate you, you goddamned bitch! (She sticks her leg out and kicks the chair over).

S: Now switch back.

Mrs RM: (Voice sounds much weaker now) I-I guess I didn't show you much love. I really felt it, but I was unhappy and bitter. You know all I had to go through with your father and brother... You were the only one I could talk to. I'm sorry...I wanted you to be happy...I wanted so much for you.

Mrs RS: You sure did!...I know you did love me, Mother, I know you were unhappy (voice much softer now, but sounding real, not whiny or mechanical). I guess I did some things that were wrong, too. I was always trying to keep you off my back.

Mrs RM: Yes, you were pretty sarcastic to me, too. And that hurt.

Mrs RS: I wish you had told me. I didn't think you were hurt at all.

Mrs RM: Well, that's all over now.

Mrs RS: Yeah, it is. I guess there's no use blaming you. You're not around anymore.

S: Can you forgive your mother now?

Mrs RS: Mother, I forgive you…I really do forgive you, (starts crying again, but not in the whiny way of before. She sounds genuinely grieving and cries for a couple of minutes).

S: Now switch back.

Mrs RM: I forgive you too, dear. You have to go on now. You can't keep blaming me forever. I made my mistakes but you have your own family and you are doing okay.

S: Do you feel ready to say goodbye now?

Mrs RS: Yes. I-I think so (starts to sob). Goodbye, Mother, goodbye (breaks down, cries for a few minutes).

S: What do you experience now?

Mrs R: I feel better. I feel…kind of relieved, like a weight is off my back. I feel calm.

S: Now that you've said goodbye to her, to this dead person, can you go around and say hello to the live people here, to the group?

Mrs. R: Yes, I'd like that.

(She goes around the room, greets people, touches some, embraces others. Many in the group are tearful. When she reaches her husband, she starts crying again, and tells him she loves him, and they embrace).

This is a perfect example of the method.

Method VII: Ann Sayre Wiseman's Guide to Working with Dreams

Ann Sayre Wiseman, an Art and Dream Therapist working in Boston, says that to explore dreams, creativity and the possible self, it is necessary to balance the conflicting voices inside, to befriend the inner orphan and to transform negative energy into a creative resource for healing and change. She has a simple and effective guide to work with dreams.

These are the 21 steps that make up the guide, and can amplify the gifts from your dream:

1. Consider that your dream mind may be giving you a gift, counsel, insights, options, or another point of view. Record dreams as soon as possible—at least capture those images, (no matter how strange, contrary or impossible the dream seems, don't let your waking mind do any editing).
2. Note the feeling the dream left you with before you judge it with your waking mind.
3. Note names, numbers, places, animals and objects. They

may be a clue to the time-line of the memory or dream content.

4. Find the metaphor. Advice or a useful observation may come in a masked device, word play, double meaning, or paradox.
5. Note the day's events which may have triggered this dream. Note fears.
6. Ask what is needed to alleviate those feelings? (This may be the work you need to do).
7. Note who or what brought you the message. What triggered recognition, awareness, realization?
8. Investigate closed containers (try to enter by means of meditation. Ask what could be inside? What is it that is being kept from my seeing or knowing?).
9. From a position of safety, confront the enemy, dialogue with the threatening power, person or situation. Ask, why have you come.
10. Do not kill the enemy, confront it, regain your power, negotiate agreement. (Win-win whenever possible.) The enemy always has something to teach us.
11. If fear woke you, return to the scene in your mind. Explore options. Ask what needs to happen to make this scene right for you.
12. In the dream space you can empower yourself; simply imagine it, If you don't know how, borrow the wisdom

of someone who does. You are creator-director-performer.

13. Note the emotional investment you deposit in your images and the projections you put on other people. (What you project on others may be a part of yourself you only recognize in others. It takes one to know one!)
14. Observe the age of your 'dream feeling'. That will help to locate the source of the feeling, the origin of the assumption, or the cause of the attitude which the dream has given you.
15. Write your dream in a short paragraph. Translate each image, person, and thing, into its 'essence' quality (for instance: what is your 'essence' translation of Mother=Safety? Model? Critic? Protector? Competitor?).
16. Re-write the dream story using these new words. It will tell you more than you thought you knew. It may become a poem.
17. Make a glossary of your images and 'essence words', (note how your dreams use, and re-use them).
18. Do not kill the enemy, confront it, regain your power, negotiate agreement. Acknowledge dream gifts.
19. Translate the 'dream story' using key words in place of people and images.

20. As you repair your position in the dream, note the discrepancies which made you the victim. Use them as a guide for self-empowering practice.
21. Give the dream a title. Date and draw symbols. Map the dream as a play on a paper-stage (using torn coloured papers and glue), so you can refer to it visually as the observer-director.

Everything you do symbolically is a rehearsal for real life. Exercise your imagination. Dreams help us clarify our polarized attitudes, opening a path to regaining balance in our lives.

Death and dying in dreams can indicate new beginnings as well as endings, of eras, feelings and relationships. Death is not necessarily an omen, it can be interpreted as a warning or a statement of urgency. Sometimes death in a dream is preparing you for the inevitable, or forcing you to consider the possibility, in preparation for facing it consciously. Death may also be telling you how angry you feel. Consider death from all angles.

Consider pain and fear in dreams as an opportunity for growth, a way to focus on issues and areas which the inner observer thinks you need to strengthen. We are capable of anything we can imagine, even though we do not act upon it in waking life.

Dreams provide a safe way to experience feelings that are too frightening to acknowledge yet. Dreams are a way to rehearse feelings and actions before daring to try them in waking life. We can practice self-empowering strategies and self-defense by programming our dreams.

Dreams are the sleeping artist in us all, a path to our own wisdom, our own best counsel, as well as an abundant source of originality.

4

Unravelling the Mystery of Incubation

Our dream journey now takes us to the sixth century BC, to the ancient cultures of Egypt, Rome and especially, Greece. For this is where, in temples the oracles presided, the mysterious and sacred ritual of incubation was prasticed. Dream incubation was the ritual of going to sleep in a sacred place in anticipation of receiving a divinely inspired dream. It was a powerful process used in these ancient cultures, primarily for healing but also for seeking guidance from the divine.

From the sixth century BC to the sixth century AD, the Greeks and Romans practised dream incubation, or going to a sacred place in order to receive a useful dream from a god. The dreamer might have asked for divine instructions for a problem in masonry, or a remedy for sterility, or for a diagnosis and cure of other ailments. He would go to one of the several hundred temples of Aesculapius or Asklepios (Ullman and Zimmerman 1979); there he would chant with the priests, abstain from wine, sexual intercourse, and certain foods that were believed to hinder dream production, and undertake some ritual bathing for purification. Then, after having been invited in a first dream by the god, he would spend the night in the abaton, lying on the bloody skins of the recently sacrificed sheep and oxen and sacred snakes of the temple for company. With all this preparation and expectation it is not surprising that he would have a significant dream. Evidently, many healings took place. Stelae (ancient upright stone columns bearing inscriptions) found at Epidaurus describe the diseases of 70 patients and the dreams that cured them. If, however, the pilgrim had an obscure dream, he could go to one of the local entrepreneurs in dream interpretation. At Memphis, the plaque over one such shopkeeper's door read: 'I interpret dreams, having the god's mandate to do so.'

In other examples cited in literature with regard to the mystery of incubation, especially that of the dream temples of the Greek god, Asklepios (Garfield, 1991), a person with an illness would go to sleep in the temple. Asklepios would appear in a dream to perform a symbolic operation or simply diagnose the illness and prescribe treatment, which the designated temple attendant, called therapeutes, would subsequently administer. Many testimonies concerning the healings and prescriptions which occurred in the dreams of those who slept in the sanctuaries of Asklepios exist today. The origins of some modern therapeutic methods have been attributed to these incubations.

Muslims continue the practice of the induced dream, but not in mosques. They call it *istiqâra*. A person with a difficult problem recites a special prayer recommended by Prophet Mohammed and then goes to sleep, expecting to receive the answer or solution in a dream. The traveller does this on the eve of a trip, the author before writing, or the statesman before an important policy decision.

In the USA, the practice of incubation is prevalent amongst various tribes of Native American Indians. Their use of dream incubation has not been limited to healing. In fact, many of their most significant cultural treasures are attributed to dreams received through incubation rituals.

For example, some Native American Indian tribes use incubation in connection with the rite of passage into adulthood. Among the Ojibwa of the Great Lakes, a young person would go out into the wilderness and prepare a ritual nest where he or she would remain, fasting, until the anticipated dream was received. Usually, their dream would contain some representative of the spirit world, who would appear and bless the young person by revealing the youth's particular gifts and abilities, and would give instructions in the use of supernatural aids which might be available to the person in the future. After being blessed by the dream, the young adult also would incur the responsibility of applying the gifts in a prescribed manner for the benefit of the community, often on penalty of contracting an untreatable illness.

In modern times, dream psychologists use different approaches. In this chapter, we will describe three methods which are practical and effective. Dream incubation as practised today is the evoking of a dream as a response to some question or concern that we present to the unconscious before we go to bed. Many of us, at least once in our lives, have gone to sleep with a problem, or a need for a new idea, clearly in mind. You say to yourself, 'Let me sleep on this problem.' You find that you often wake up with a solution. You discover that this method sometimes works. With dream incubation, it is possible to make it work most of the time, and it is an easy method to master. By using any of the three methods that are discussed below, you can incubate your first dream tonight.

Dream incubation is not necessarily obtaining an answer through a dream to a specific question. A great deal depends on how well you hone the question and how much pre-dream work you have undertaken on the problem itself. However, you will almost certainly find a connection between the question and the message of the dream. The only exception will be if the unconscious feels that you have a higher priority, which has to be dealt with first. For example, you may incubate a problem at work but you may still not have dealt with a relationship that has suddenly ended at home, which the unconscious decides is of greater priority. Of course, the dream is like a prism and can deal with several issues simultaneously. But it requires a very competent dream therapist to be able to discern how many different issues the dream is dealing with.

Method I: The Basic Approach

In order to use this method, select something that you would like to bring into your life. It could be the answer to a problem that is troubling you at work, or with a relationship. Perhaps you would like to improve your health, your state of mind, or resolve a recurring nightmare. Maybe you would like creative inspiration or an insight into how to pursue one of your personal goals. What is important is that you truly want whatever you select and that you will honestly appreciate and make use of it once it comes. Incubation is a powerful process and should be given appropriate respect. For the purpose of this experiment, try to find something that applies directly to your life right now.

In incubating a dream, we immerse ourselves in the problem we have chosen, by thinking about it and opening it up to all possibilities. Then, as we sleep, we stay with the problem, repeating it to ourselves, or focus it more on a question which we repeat as we fall asleep. As we relate to our dreams more fully, this level of dream incubation can be almost a nightly occurrence.

Thus, the fervency or passion by which one makes the request to the dream source determines the response one receives. There must be a concentration of energy and feeling, an openness to personal need, character traits of sincerity and integrity, and a receptivity to the dream.

Sit on the side of your bed and quieten both body and mind. Next, hold your question or problem clearly in mind for a few minutes. Then lie down. As you are falling asleep, gently ask yourself to have (and clearly remember) a dream that reveals the answer as either an insight, an actual experience, or both. As you drift off to sleep, keep your question in mind, trusting that the exercise will be successful. If other thoughts distract you, return to your incubation focus.

The moment you awaken, whether in the morning or during the night, record any thoughts that you have had. At this point, do not judge content. Simply record what you remember. After you get up, read and reflect upon any thoughts that you recorded, and make whatever associations, interpretations, and waking life connections that you can.

The answer may or may not be obvious, but trust that the process is working regardless, and try to put any insights you receive into practice. This last step may involve facing personal fears or overcoming personal limitations. Try to maintain a grateful appreciation for any guidance you receive, as it will most likely promote further insight and future success.

Even if you do not remember too much of the dream or have little success, rest assured that your incubation has had an effect. It may simply be simmering on unconscious levels and may come to you as a sudden revelation or as an insight to act upon during the day, though you may not connect such a moment with your incubation at all.

Method II: The Delaney Way

Gayle Delaney (1979) has developed what she calls 'phrase focusing', or secular incubation. Phrase focusing dream incubation is secular in that it is meant to be part of the normal everyday life of the dreamer.

The method is relatively brief, requires no therapist or guide and quite consistently results in useful dream responses. Those who use this method could believe that they receive dream answers from deeper parts of themselves, or from a divine power separate from themselves. Dreamers may direct their petitions, therefore, to their inner, higher, unconscious selves. Gayle Delaney believes that this method of dream incubation will enable you to find new resources in the development of your strengths, talents and inner life on your own. There will be occasions when your incubated dreams answer your questions in very little terms that will need no interpretation. Sometimes, these dreams will provide you with an experience of insight or understanding that in itself will give you your answer, or aid in the resolution of your problem. Other dreams may need exploration if you are to benefit fully from their meaning.

You can incubate a dream on any problem or question that concerns you. In choosing your incubation issue, be careful that it is one you are really willing to explore, because if it is not, you will be likely to forget any dreams you may have about it.

There are seven steps in Delaney's incubation method:

Step I: Choose the right night; a night when you are not very tired. It is important that you do not take alcohol or drugs. Even certain sleeping pills affect dreaming. Most users who take an active interest in their dream life, find that they no longer need them. Be sure to spend ten to twenty uninterrupted minutes just before sleeping to work on your dream journal. And then, you will need at least ten minutes the following morning to record your incubated dream, unless you awaken in the middle of the night and record it.

Step II: Day notes. Before going to sleep, record your day notes, that is, events that have occurred during the day. The main purpose is to summarize your day's thoughts, feelings and actions. Recording your thoughts and feelings of the day down on paper will clear your mind, relax you, and help you to be in a proper state to sleep.

Step III: Lights! (Incubation discussion). If you were directing a movie, you would call for lights to illuminate and highlight the set. In this step you use your conscious mind and heart to take a close look at the various aspects of your situation. Ask yourself whether you are really ready to examine the problem, called the incubation issue. Discuss the matter thoroughly with yourself, writing down as much of the discussion as possible.

Step IV: Incubation phrase. On the next line in your journal, write down a one line question or request that expresses your deepest and clearest desire to understand the dynamics of your predicament. This will be your incubation phrase. Make it simple. You may want to play around with several phrases until you find the one that feels best. For example, your incubation phrase might be, 'Help me understand, why I am afraid of heights and what I can do about it.' Or, 'What are the dynamics of the relationship between X and me?'

Step V: Focus! Camera! Now you are ready to place your journal beside your bed, turn off the lamp, and close your eyes. Having done this, focus all your attention on your incubation phrase. Imagine that you are about to begin production of a dream scene that will answer your question. You direct the camera to zero in on a close-up of your main point of interest, your incubation phrase. As you lie in bed, repeat the phrase over and over to yourself. As you fall asleep, forget about the written ruminations of your incubation discussion. Concentrate on your question. If distracting thoughts occur, such as, 'Will this work?' or 'Tomorrow I must remember to...,' let them go. Keep bringing your focus back to the incubation phrase, which is the distillation of your query. Let all your feelings focus on this phrase. Keep it in your mind up to the very last second before you fall asleep.

Step VI: Action! This step is the easiest. Just sleep. In ways we do not understand, a portion of our consciousness that usually appears unconscious from the point of view of the waking self, will make contact with sources of experience and wisdom most often available only in the sleeping state. As we quiet the daytime barrage of sense perceptions and fall asleep, we tune into a subtler level of experience.

Step VII: Record. Record in detail all your dream memories as soon as you awaken, whether it is in the middle of the night or in the morning. Make no judgments at this point regarding the relevance of the dreams or pieces of dreams you recall to your incubation question. Include any feelings, thoughts, songs, or fantasies that come to mind. Try to re-experience the dream.

If you have time, jot down any associations that come to

mind regarding different dream elements, and sketch unusual images in the margin. In the commentary section of your journal, keeping your incubation phrase in mind, make an attempt to draw meaning from your dream.

Method III: The Menezes Incubation Ceremony

Over the last 25 years of working with dreams, I have developed a unique incubation ceremony that is held on the evening prior to my dream workshops. The participants have included managers, scientists, priests and nuns, housewives, small entrepreneurs, businessmen and professionals. My colleagues from the Indian Association for the Study of Dreams have also helped me to test and fine-tune the design and application of the incubation ceremony, which has produced excellent results in terms of dreams and dream recall. It is a step-by-step approach and I have discovered that participants find the experience very powerful. This method is especially meant to be used with dream groups.

Here is how it works:

Before the participants arrive for the incubation ceremony they are asked to bathe and to wear loose clothing. We gather in a separate room prior to the incubation ceremony, where we talk to the participants about dreams and the ancient history of incubation. We tell them about the four key characteristics of dreams and give them practical hints to recall and record their dreams. The incubation room itself is closed, and participants have to remove their footwear before entering it.

The incubation room is prepared for the ceremony in the following way:

1. The room must have the right kind of energy to facilitate the relaxation of the participants.
2. We try to create the atmosphere of a sacred space.
3. We put rock salt in a bucket of water and wash the floor of the room to get rid of negative energy.
4. A pranic healer, a Reiki master, or a meditator spends time in the room to create the right vibrations.
5. Sandalwood *agarbattis* (incense sticks) are lit.
6. Soft instrumental music, usually Indian, is played in the background as the incubants enter the room and settle down on the floor.

Preparing the Incubants

Next, I speak to the group about the incubation process in a soft and quiet tone of voice, with my eyes closed, as follows:

I would like you to quickly go through all the problems that you are facing, all your concerns, all the things that are bothering you and creating stress for you. See them in a grand sweep. Don't dwell on any one at this moment. Let them move past you, as on a screen.

Now you can look at the thoughts as they move more slowly and you can try to prioritize your problems and your concerns. On top, the problem which is causing you the greatest concern or stress. Then, the next one, and the next one, and so on... Check again if the number one priority is truly the most important. If it is, look at it more closely from all angles. Ask yourself 'Am I really ready to confront the problem, to deal with it, or do I have a hidden investment to let it continue? Am I getting something out of this situation?' (For example: if I continue being an alcoholic, I can continue avoiding responsibilities).

This is the time to ask yourself, How did the problem begin? Can you remember? And then what happened? And then what happened? And so on... Reflect on what would happen if the problem is solved. Are you ready for that eventuality? Can you handle it? In your mind, run through the whole history of the problem.

Now look at the various alternatives available to you to solve the problem. The more alternatives you come up with, the more creative you are, and the more freedom you will give yourself to find a solution.

The next step is to weigh the alternatives. Each alternative solution comes with a price in terms of the consequences. Are you ready to pay the price, to face the consequences?

Now use your pad and pen and begin scribbling your thoughts and feelings as they come with regard to the problem. Nothing rational or logical. Just let the pen flow in a burst of energy. Let the pen do the writing on its own.

(After about 10 minutes) Stop. By this time, working on the problem, you may have even abandoned what you thought was your original problem and identified the real one. That's all right. That's what happens sometimes. Now write down your question, carefully honed to make it clear, on a piece of paper. Make it short and simple. You are asking the question of the greatest 'computer' in the world. Remember, if you put rubbish in, you will get rubbish out.

Fold your piece of paper, with the question on it, and place it in the envelope given to you. Before you go to bed, place the envelope under your pillow. This is just a simple psychological device. But it works. It will help you to focus on the question which is what you will be encouraged to do from now on.

We will be putting off the lights during the last part of the incubation. So lie down and make yourself comfortable, ensure that you have your own space and you are not touching anybody else.

Complete Instructions for the Incubation

We will now begin the process of complete relaxation. I will give you instructions so please listen to them attentively.

Lie down on your back with your arms a little away from the body and the palms facing upwards. The legs should be slightly apart. It is the position adopted in *shavasana*. Close your eyes and keep them closed during the entire Incubation. Take a deep breath and as you breathe out, feel the cares and the worries of the day flow out of you. Become aware of the existence of the physical body lying on the floor. Be aware of your body lying in perfect stillness. Become aware of all the points where your body meets the floor. Become aware of your natural breath. Do not interfere with the natural process.

Let us rotate the consciousness. Rotation of the consciousness is simply moving the awareness by taking a trip through the different parts of the body. Very quickly, let the awareness go from part to part.

First, move your awareness to the base of your spine. Remember, this is where your *mooladhara chakra* is situated, the point where all your stress has been accumulated over the years. Breathe deeply and slowly, then let go. Now, move up to that part of the spine which is in line with your navel area. Here is where your *manipura chakra* is situated. Here is where all your emotions reside. Breathe deeply and let go. Now, slowly move up your spine in line with your heart. This is the seat of *anahat chakra*. Breathe deeply and slowly let go. Let your consciousness move from doubt to trust. Breathe deeply. Now, move up the spine in level with your throat. Here is the *vishudhi chakra*. Breathe deeply and let go. As this *chakra* opens up, you have the ability to express yourself totally.

We will play you some soft music that has been especially chosen to help you relax even further. Now begin to feel your body getting heavier and heavier, and slowly sinking into the floor. Keep your focus on the question in your envelope. (The music is played. There are two long pauses in between. During each pause I tell them to focus on the question in the envelope.) When the music slowly fades away, I ask the incubants to get out of their relaxation very, very slowly. A single light is switched on.

The Menezes Dream Incubation Ritual can be very effective as these two experiences illustrate:

Saying Goodbye to Mother Teresa

Zenobia, a middle-aged woman from a business family, stood up at the end of the incubation and announced, 'With due apologies to Mother Teresa, I have cancelled her out of my life.' Zenobia disclosed that all her adult life she perceived herself as being like Mother Teresa—sacrificing her life to doing good deeds for others. While introducing herself at the beginning of the workshop, she had drawn a picture of herself as Mother Teresa. During the incubation it became clearer to her that this behaviour only fed her ego and was the source of her problems. In deep relaxation, she saw her hand very firmly cancelling out Mother Teresa from the picture she had drawn. 'I thanked her, of course,' said Zenobia, 'but I told her firmly that I was dropping her from my life. It was creating too much misery for me and for everyone else.' A major change had occurred in her life.

Stan's Breakthrough

Stan Lobo, a young engineer from the R&D centre of a medium-size company, was working on a new combustion system called the pulse combustor. With the increasing size of the boilers and the easy availability of a variety of fuels in the market, his company faced a great deal of competition. Consequently, the management wanted R&D to create a compact and efficient boiler, in which the fuel undergoes complete combustion and the heat given is more or less completely absorbed. Prior to his incubation, Lobo's focus was on how to develop a diaphragm made of a substance that had elastic and metallic properties, so that it could act as a diode. During his incubation, Stan Lobo had a breakthrough, and later created a diaphragm that met his company's requirements.

Method IV: Henry Reed's Incubation

Henry Reed (1994), who describes himself as an independent scholar of psychology, was convinced that the ancient method of incubation could be used in modern times for healing to take place in a dream by a god through the visitation of a spirit. He reconstructed the ritual of dream incubation at the C.J. Jung Institute in Zurich. At a summer camp for young adults, he tried an experiment, by setting up an aesthetically pleasing dome-shaped tent to serve as the dream sanctuary. The 'dream tent' was to be the focus of his efforts to recreate a dream incubation ceremony. He used modern symbols and procedures to place today's incubant in an approximately equivalent frame of mind as presumably existed in the dream incubants of the historical past.

His procedure was composed of four segments:

1. Selecting the Dreamer for Incubation: In the temple of Aesculapius, a dream incubation could not be sought until the person had been guided to seek such an experience in a prior dream. To maintain the strong factor of self-selection, Henry Reed insisted there was no solicitation. He asked potential incubants to rely on their dreams to provide the final basis of self-selection.
2. Preparing the Incubant: After the dreamer had an invitational dream to participate in the incubation ritual, a date was picked for the ceremony, usually one to three days later. In the interim, Reed discussed the details of the preparation with the incubant. It was the most

important aspect of the ritual. It involved the incubants contemplating the purpose of the incubation, choosing the personal symbols of the sacred place and the revered benefactor. They would also develop pictures representing these symbols and the dream from which the decision to incubate had been based. Finally, usually 24 hours before the incubation ceremony, they would spend some time in symbolic purification.

3. Incubation Ceremony: In the early evening, Reed and the incubant would meet in the dream tent, spending a few minutes in silence together before beginning the ritual. Reed would then ask the incubant to explain his purpose. He would specifically ask about the sources of intensives and inhibitions to achieve the purpose of the incubation. This period of the ceremony, lasting about two to four hours, functions as an opportunity for cathartic confession, prompting the activation prior to sleep of many of the ideas and feelings associated with the incubant's purpose for this dream quest. He would then work on the dream that had brought the incubant to the ceremony.
4. The Testimony Session: The morning after the ceremony, Reed would return to the dream tent, where the incubant had spent the night alone. Reed would hear the dreams of the incubant at least twice and then ask

about their possible meanings. As the last step, the incubant would prepare a written testimony of the incubation ritual, beginning the account with his first contact with Reed.

Finally, Reed asked the incubant to present him with a symbolic gift; forgiving the incubant of any obligation to him, appeasing any desire of Reed's for compensation and ending their ritual relationship as incubant and therapeutes.

Dream Incubation and Yoga Nidra

Some practitioners of *Yoga Nidra* ask me the difference between *Yoga Nidra* and incubation. As Swami Satyananda Saraswati, who perfected the technique, explained, '*Yoga Nidra* belongs to the hypnogogic state between waking and dreaming, where a distinct and important band of awareness and experience lies.' *Yoga Nidra* occurs at this threshold of sense consciousness and sleep consciousness. It is entered by learning to extend the duration of the short hypnogogic state which precedes normal sleep. According to Swami Satyananda(1976):

Research has shown that during this period, the sense modalities are disengaged systematically in a fixed order as the awareness is internally directed towards the deeper levels of the mind. According to tantric philosophy, this entry into sleep can be understood as the progressive withdrawal of the awareness back through the *chakras* towards its cosmic source (*sahasra*). For example, according to research, the sense of smell (olfaction) is the first sense to disengage. In tantra, this corresponds to *mooladhara chakra* and the earth *tattwa* or element. Smell is followed by taste (gustation), corresponding to the *swadhishthan chakra* and the *tattwa* of the water. After taste, visual capacity, which is the modality *(tanmatra)* of *manipura chakra*, disappears, then touch (*anahata*, air element), and finally hearing (*vishidhi*, *akasha* or ether element). We can now understand that *Yoga Nidra*, in which awareness of the verbal instructions alone remains, corresponds to a state of sleep at the very borderline between wakefulness and dreaming.

5

The Rainbow of Dream Experience

Let us imagine, for a moment, that our odyssey has brought us to a winding road on a mountainside. The breeze is cool, for it has just rained, and the scent of pine trees fills the air. As you turn the corner, you notice with surprise a huge rainbow that appears on the horizon. It is like the rainbow of your dream experience—a myriad of colours and hues, merged into one another. Each colour and hue has its own significance. There are dreams which bring you good fortune, like a pot of gold at the end of the rainbow. There are dreams which predict the future. There are dreams which talk of a past life that has been forgotten. There are dreams that recur to jog you into paying attention. And there are simple dreams of ordinary, mundane life.

In this chapter we will discuss nine different types:

1. Housekeeping dreams
2. Psychological problem-solving dreams
3. Recurring dreams

4. Telepathic dreams
5. Precognitive dreams
6. Messages from the other shore
7. Sexual dreams
8. Past-life dreams
9. Colourpuncture and dreams

Housekeeping Dreams

Nothing in a dream is trivial. The source, or the unconscious that produces the dream, is very miserly. It utilizes every bit of space on the canvas on which your dream has been painted in a meaningful way. Dreams vary greatly in their importance, depending on what is going on in the dreamer's life, or more specifically, in his mind. Sometimes, if you have gone to sleep with several 'kitchen issues' that are not completed, the dream may simply be cleaning up, tying up loose ends. These are called housekeeping dreams. In such dreams you might discover where you have misplaced your keys or spectacles. Or, that the nagging feeling you had before going to bed was because you had forgotten to take out the garbage!

Psychological Problem-Solving Dreams

There are numerous ways in which dreams help us to solve our personal problems. They deal with a whole range of them in the most fascinating and mysterious of ways. Such dreams help to reduce, if not dissipate, fear, anxiety, stress and gloom. They struggle with conflicts of all kinds, in relationships, career choices, moral dilemmas or, even the choice of a spiritual path. Some dream psychologists believe that dreams arise only when there are conflicts. This is not true. Dreaming is a much more complex and deeper phenomenon. Dreams reflect our own preoccupations to us and are a response to our conscious need for a solution to a particular problem. The answers are delayed because we are not yet ready to face them.

Many years ago, when a relationship ended, I took my broken heart and withdrew to the hills in Kalimpong. During the week that I was there, I watched the unconscious, night after night, slowly and carefully mending my heart—easing the pain, dwelling on the good times, converting the sorrow into hope of a new day, until, in the final dream I had, when I dozed off during the afternoon on the flight home, there was reconciliation and joy.

Life can be seen as a series of meetings and partings, of learning encounters, where we can make discoveries about ourselves if we are open to the experience. Dreams deal with the intricacies of each encounter, and the resources we have to cope with them. A dream is a personal document, a letter to oneself. Dreams reveal what we really think of ourselves when the mask of waking life is removed. Dreams also reveal how the dreamer conceives of other people, even if he does not acknowledge this in the waking state. A dominating boss could appear as a bull; a placid, lazy one as a cow. Dreams cut through the pretensions and deceits of daily life and lay bare the true feelings we have of people. That is why, according to Ullman, 'dreams never lie'.

Recurring Dreams

There are two reasons why dreams recur. The first is that images and emotions connected with a particularly important event in the past recur when the dreamer faces a similar problem later in life. We all have emotional residues from our past that we have not quite disposed of; particular areas of vulnerability that get bruised from time to time. When such an event occurs, one generally has a dream which depicts the problem and where we are in relation to it. These are known as 'recurrent dreams'.

For example, a young boy who is very anxious about his exam may dream the previous night that he has got his subjects mixed up and that he faces a crisis in the examination hall. He wakes up in panic. Later, when he is 40, and has to make an important presentation to his boss, the same feelings of anxiety could recur, triggering off the old exam dream of his youth.

Another common recurring dream is of chasing a train. Some manage to catch it, others just miss it. Such dreams often occur when people are experiencing great anxiety with regard to deadlines. It may be work-related or it may be marriage related, as the following dream illustrates:

Papa Knows Best

> I am going on a train journey with my wife and son. She is constantly warning me not to get off the train and get left behind. I ignore her and am busy chatting and laughing with the other passengers, who are all strangers. I get off the train at a small station, and wander off towards the exit gate. The ticket collector at the gate tells me the train is about to start, but I see a metal object on the ground and am trying to set it right. The ticket collector urges me to leave it alone and run and catch the train. I run behind the train, and manage to get into the last bogey, where my wife is waiting for me.

This dream had recurred several times, but this was the first time that the dreamer had managed, just in time, to catch the train. He ascribed the change in the dream to a recent realization that he should pay more attention to his wife and child. When he worked on the dream, he discovered that the ticket collector, who urged him to catch the train, was his dead father—conveying a powerful message.

'What the hell are your doing?'

The second reason why dreams recur is because the unconscious wants to bring something important to the dreamer's attention. The dream, as it were, is knocking at his door. For instance, a young man dreamt that he was travelling in a suburban train and that it was going at great speed, even though there was a red light signal in front and another train coming in the opposite direction. Just in time, both the trains stop. The driver of the oncoming train puts his head out of the window and shouts, 'Hey, what the hell are you doing?'

The young dreamer immediately understood the meaning of the dream. He woke up and exclaimed aloud, 'I'm marrying the wrong girl!' Apparently, he was being forced into a traditional marriage by his parents who were opposed to his relationship with the woman who lived in the United States. The dream warned him, and helped him make the right choice.

The Mystery Child

An interesting variation is the experience of Karuna, a school teacher in her thirties. The dream began when she was 14 years old, and lasted till she got married at the age of 22. Here is how she re-tells her experience:

> When I was about 14 years old, I used to have a recurring dream: I am holding a very beautiful child of around eight

> or nine months old in my arms. The most remarkable feature of the child were his eyes. They sparkled with intelligence. As I held the child close to me, I used to have long adult conversations with him about any problem that I faced during the day. The child responded with advice which always helped me to deal with the problems in my waking hours. The remarkable thing about these dreams was that whenever I saw them, I never forgot any part of the conversation when I woke up. The settings of my dreams were never the same—sometimes it was a public garden, other times a hotel or a cinema theatre, at times it was the railway station or even the house I lived in at that time.

Even though she had many friends and acquaintances, Karuna found it difficult to confide her innermost thoughts to her peers. She created the baby, like a doll, with whom she could safely share her secrets. It seems as if the responses of the baby came from the source itself; a direct connection between God and child.

Telepathic Dreams

Telepathic dreams occur when a dreamer appears to absorb information about an event while it is happening, even though he is a considerable distance away from the scene. It is as if the dreamer is reading the mind of another person while he is undergoing considerable stress or trauma or is in a dangerous situation. There are many reports of people dreaming of the death of someone at the precise time it happened.

Let us look at some cases:

The Call from New York

A family in India made their weekly phone call to Jagdish, a younger son who lived in Washington, DC. As usual, they took turns talking to him, just prior to the Fourth of July weekend. A couple of hours later, however, the mother woke up with a start from her sleep to say that she had dreamt that Jagdish was seriously ill and in a hospital. She refused to be mollified by the other members of the family, who pointed out that they had just spoken to him and that he seemed to be fine. On her insistence, they called him again but he was not at home. Later in the day, they received a call from New York to say that Jagdish, on his way to the city to celebrate Independence Day, had met with an accident. He was in a hospital in New York.

The Nuclear Family

A scientist attending a workshop in Pune, dreamt that her son was in hospital in Kochi, Kerala. She saw the hospital bed where he lay with a bandage around his left ankle. In the morning, she called her husband, who was also a scientist. Her husband confirmed what she had seen in the dream—that the son was indeed in the hospital. The boy had fallen off his bicycle and had been admitted to the hospital at exactly the same time the mother had the dream. He had been injured, and his left ankle was bandaged exactly the way she had seen it in her dream.

Yogesh and Molly

Yogesh Ketkar (his real name), is a young automobile engineer. At the age of nine, Yogesh pestered his mother to buy him a fish tank. However, since she could not afford it, she bought him a large jar instead, where he kept his collection of five fish. Yogesh says:

> One night I dreamt that my black Molly was seriously ill and sticking to a corner of the jar and gasping for breath. Sure enough, when I awoke and went to check she was exactly where the dream had shown her. I gave her some medicine and went back to bed. She seemed fine the next day. A week later I dreamt that the black Molly was dead. When I went to the tank to feed the fish the next morning, I found that the fish had indeed died in the night. The strange feeling still stays with me to this day.

Research on Dream Telepathy

A great deal of research was carried out in this field during the last century in England, by the Founders of the Society for

Cyclical Research. The research findings were later reported in a book titled *Phantasms of the Living* in 1886 (Ullman et al., 1988).

Dream telepathy has also been studied in the sleep laboratory. In a series of well-designed experiments at the Maimonides Hospital in New York in the 1960s, Ullman and Krippner found evidence of a telepathic effect occurring in the dream state. A receiver (dreamer) was wired up and woken after each REM period to give an account of any dreams. Each time the receiver was dreaming, an awake sender tried to influence the dreams of the subject by concentrating on certain material that had been randomly selected. Different target material was selected over the several nights of the experiment. 'Blind' judges later rated the amount of association between the materials—in this case famous paintings—and the dreams of the targets. In one study, the sender focused on a specific painting each night, such as *Yellow Rabi* by Chagall or *School of the Dance* by Degas. The dreamer caught five of the seven paintings right.

In 1983, I participated in an experiment in telepathic dreams conducted by Robert Van de Castle, at the Second International Conference of the Association for the Study of Dreams held at the University of Virginia, Charlottesville. The target (the person who was to be the focus of our dreams) was asked not to tell us anything about her problem. This was part of the experimental design, to avoid any influence. Van de Castle asked the target to lend each of us a personal belonging as a token—a handkerchief, trinket, a watch—which we had to place under our pillow with the intention of dedicating our dream to the solution of her problem.

The next morning, we shared our dreams. Some members of the group felt their dreams connected with the target's problem. My dream initially seemed to have nothing to do with the target. It featured a busy sidewalk in New York and other such mundane scenes. Curiously, however, throughout my dream, a Native American wearing his traditional headgear kept popping up in the crowd. It had no relevance to my dream. When the target person shared her dream, I was amazed. She dreamt that she had climbed a steep mountain to meet a wise man who lived on the top and who would give her the solution to her problem. The wise man turned out to be a Native American who was wearing the traditional headdress. He gave her a message that she felt was the solution to her problem. Later, the group made a collage which the target found very useful.

Pre-cognitive Dreams

Just two weeks before his assassination, Abraham Lincoln dreamt that there was a funeral at the White House (Delaney,

1979). In the dream he asked a soldier who the person in the casket was. The soldier replied, 'the President of the United States'. Later, when he told his wife about the dream, she remarked that he would die in office. Similarly, Mark Twain had a very real dream where he saw his brother in a casket (Delaney, 1979). Less than a week later, his brother was killed in an explosion. Upon arriving at the town where it took place, he saw his brother laid out in a casket—just as in his dream.

After the *Titanic* tragedy in 1912, when it sank in the Atlantic Ocean, there were reports of at least two dozen people who cancelled their trip because of precognitive dreams they had about the sinking. There was one businessman who had the same precognitive dream about the sinking of the *Titanic* three times. However, he chose to ignore the warning, until a sudden business exigency forced him to cancel!

Precognitive dreams are those which appear to anticipate a later unexpected event, which could not reasonably have been inferred from information available to the dreamer at the time of the dream. Often, premonitions appear in the form of dreams, although some people may also experience them in the waking state.

Throughout all of human history, there have been reports of premonition dreams. The most famous one being 'The dream of the Pharaoh,' which Joseph interpreted. It is believed that, as a result of Joseph's interpretation of seven fat and seven thin cattle, as meaning seven years of plenty followed by seven years of famine, the Pharaoh took action. He built up food stocks and saved his people. Many clay tablets have been discovered in cuneiform script reporting precognitive dreams by the ancient Assyrians and Babylonians. The ancient Egyptians, Greeks and even the Roman civilization gave credence to precognitive dreams.

Dr Hearne (LaBerge, 1985) conducted extensive research into premonitions after he experienced an accident while travelling on a ferry, which he apparently had pre-knowledge of. His research concludes that people who experience premonitions are mainly females, and they mostly concern unexpected events that will happen to people close to the dreamer.

Foretelling Your Death

The executive director of a large public sector corporation in Baroda, India, shared the following dream at one of my creativity workshops:

> I am near a window and am knocking at it to get the attention of people passing by outside. They seem to ignore me. They look at me, turn their face away and move quickly. Then I notice an ambulance. A man who I think has been killed in an accident is carried on a stretcher into

> the ambulance, there is blood splattered on his clothes. I am curious and trying hard to ascertain who the victim is. Fortunately, my childhood friend Pillai is near me and I feel reassured.

Exactly a year after having this dream, the executive director died in a car accident. A truck had crashed into his car which turned turtle. It is possible that he tried to open the door, to get the attention of passers-by. Incidentally, it was Pillai, his childhood friend, who also worked in the same corporation, who rushed to the scene of the accident and extricated the body of his friend from the car.

The Green Snake of Dreams

Precognitive dreams are not only predictors of doom. In India, it is believed that such dreams can bring tidings of joy. They can also guide you to your guru. Given below is the dream of a young woman troubled by the death of her parents in quick succession.

> I am standing at the bottom of a multistoried building with my father. There is a lot of sand and concrete around me. There is a staircase leading upwards. There is a cement seat at the entrance to the building. I sit down with my father and he hands me a small green snake. I am not at all scared of it. As I lovingly hold the snake and turn it around, I see the head of the snake open up and change into the face of

> an old man in meditation. I am intrigued by the face and go on staring at it. Suddenly, I turn around to speak to my father and he is nowhere to be seen.

A month later, the young woman came to my home for a dream workshop. When I opened the door for her, she looked stunned. She stared at me, and recognized it was the face she had seen in her dream. I told her later, in jest, that Morpheus, the Greek god of dreams, is often depicted as a green serpent.

Near-Death Experience of a Salesman

There is a story narrated by the Mother of the Aurobindo Ashram at Pondicherry, (*Sri Aurobindo and the Mother*, 1971) about the salesman in France who was staying in a five-star hotel. One night he dreamt of a coffin, and that there was an elevator-boy in the hotel uniform next to it, pointing at the coffin and asking the salesman to get inside. The next morning, as he came out of his room which was on the seventh floor and reached the elevator, there was the same boy from his dream, wearing the same uniform and pointing to the elevator, and asking him to go in. The salesman said, 'No, thanks,' and took the stairs. But before he reached the ground floor, he heard the elevator crash. Later, he learnt that all the occupants had been killed.

Mother's explanation was that an entity had forewarned him. The image of the elevator-boy, she says, makes you think an intelligence, or a consciousness intervened, and forewarned him. Something in the sub-conscious was aware of it, because it was already there in the subtle physical. 'The accident already existed before it happened. That is the law of accidents.'

Messages from the Other Shore

We have already mentioned dreams wherein people who are dead appear. In interpreting such dreams, you might discover that the dead person is just a metaphor for a living person. For example, your dead father may appear in a dream but he could be a metaphor for an authority figure, such as your boss. There are dreams however, where the dead person himself is sending a clear message, usually to a loved one. Here are two such examples:

Doctor's Dilemma

Dr Shanti Patil, who had an excellent academic and professional record, fell in love with, and married Dr Ajit Sud, another well-known medical practitioner. They enjoyed a good personal and professional relationship. However, a few years into their marriage, while they were holidaying at a beach resort, Ajit went for a swim, got caught in a current and drowned. Shanti brought the body home and was quite distraught for many days. But she had to keep going for the sake of their teenage son. When she started to reorganize her life, she realized that she could not find her husband's insurance papers. Though she looked all over the house in vain. That night, she had the following dream:

> I saw my husband, very clearly. He looked as when I last saw him alive. He spoke to me directly, 'Look in the drawer where we keep the papers relating to the fax machine,' he advised.

'When I awoke in the morning, I suddenly recalled the dream. I opened the drawer, picked up the fax file, and sure enough the insurance papers were there!'

The Banker's Daughter

In another instance, Vidya Gaikwad, a management consultant and trainer, shared the following experience:

> My father was an audit manager in a large bank. He was in his mid-fifties. We were three children. Both my older sister and my younger brother were married, and lived separately. I was the only one who lived with my parents. I was my father's favourite. When I was 22 years old, my father went to a nearby town to attend a wedding. There he suffered a cardiac arrest and died. It was a great shock for me and the family.

> A few days later, when I was dozing in a hypnogogic state, (neither awake nor asleep), I saw my father. The first time I had this experience, he told me where to look for the file where he kept his share certificates. Then he said there was a mantra written on a paper and also kept in the file. It was very important that I should give it to my brother. He repeated it several times. The next time he appeared, he told me about a book in which he kept details about his finances. Nobody in the house knew that he kept such a book and we were all surprised to find it. I never saw him again.

There are two pre-conditions that appear to be necessary to receive messages from 'the other shore'. First, a strong emotional bond must exist between the dreamer and the dead person who sends the message. Second, the subject of the message must be important and urgent.

Sexual Dreams

Sex plays an important part in our lives and it would obviously play an equally important part in our dreams. Social attitudes, restraints, repression and guilt have ensured that sex occupies more space than it should, if society had a mature and relaxed way of dealing with a natural need. In more than 20 years of dreamwork experience, I have had to deal with disparate groups of people, and discovered that dreams about sex, or with vivid sexual imagery, swung from one extreme to the other.

Sometimes I worked with groups at a commune, presided over by an enlightened Master. The groups were large, about 30 people in each group, and they came from about 20 western countries. There were usually an equal number of men and women. Their sexual dreams were fairly explicit. The men often dreamt of having sex with one of the three women (dubbed the Unholy Trinity) who administered the commune. These were seen as macho or power dreams, rather than sexual dreams. The women were usually more down to earth. An English disciple, unhappy with her boyfriend's sexual prowess, dreamt that 'he was trying to push a plug into a socket, but it went half-cock'. Most of them were quite easy and comfortable talking about sex. However, the homosexuals and lesbians in the group seemed less forthcoming, even though they sat as couples and indulged in overt sexual behaviour.

The other extreme were nuns and priests who rarely brought their sexual dreams to the group. However, in one-to-one sessions, or in informal meetings, they spoke about dreams which were obviously sexual but were couched in complex, even sacred, imagery.

Balu Gets Bold

Somewhere in the middle, were corporate managers. They

often used sexual imagery to convey power struggles and conflicts. The following instance is a typical case:

Sarojini Vyas, a female manager, worked in an insurance company and had 17 agents reporting to her—all of them male. There was one particular agent, Balu, whom she disliked as a person, apart from which his performance was well below her expectations. Sarojini spent considerable time and effort to improve Balu's general appearance and work performance. Although he became more well-trained, his work was still below expectation. One night Sarojini dreamt that she was lying naked in her bed, when Balu entered, locked the door behind him. He undressed and they had sexual intercourse.

When Sarojini recalled the dream in the morning, she was literally nauseated. 'How could I have sex with that awful man?', she asked herself. But when she worked on interpreting the dream, she understood what it meant. In her words, 'I was desperate that Balu should perform for me. And that is exactly what he did in the dream. He fulfilled my wish!' she exclaimed, laughing.

Usually, a sexual dream refers to one in which both the content and the feelings are sexual in nature. Sarojini's dream is not really a sexual dream, it has more to do with the need to control a subordinate. Sexual imagery is used very often by managers who are really dealing with problems of power or powerlessness.

Often therefore, sexual dreams arise when the dreamer has been exposed to excessive sexual stimulation without consummation. Any unusual or enforced period of abstinence may result in sexual dreams. In adolescence, sexual dreams are often associated with nocturnal emissions in the male and the experience of orgasm in the female. In such dreams, the sex act is quite graphically represented. In adults, sexual needs are more indirectly dealt with and are discreetly masked.

It is important to remember that sexual imagery is used as a metaphor to express feelings of closeness and intimacy, as well as a means to avoid intimate relationships. Sometimes, people may be confused when they dream of having sexual relations with friends of the same sex. These are really the attempts of the unconscious to express the intimacy that one finds difficult to express in the waking hours. They are not sexual dreams per se. Ullman and Zimmerman (1970) suggest that the dreamer should ask:

1. Is my dream the result of unfulfilled sexual tensions?
2. Am I expressing a problem about my sexual life?
3. Am I expressing a problem about my life in sexual metaphors?

As we discussed earlier, most of our dreams occur during periods of REM sleep. During REM, men have some degree of erection 90 per cent of the time and women regularly experience some degree of vaginal vascular engorgement, clitoral swelling and increased lubrication. Do these erections and engorgements cause, or are they caused by, our sexual dreams? Apparently not in most cases. In a comprehensive study that examined 10,000 dream reports to see what normal people dream about and how often, Hall and Van de Castle (1966) found that only 12 per cent of the dreams in their sample contained overt sexual interactions.

According to Dr Lonnie Barbach (1987), a sex psychologist, men do not focus as much conflictual emotional baggage on sex as women, so it would seem likely that men's sexual dreams would be generally less conflicted. Psychiatrist Dr Loma Flowers (Delaney, 1994) observes that since men in their waking lives are less vulnerable to attack and coercion in heterosexual situations, heterosexual imagery would not likely serve to represent conflict in most men's dreams.

Kaplan-Williams (1986) has an interesting and fresh approach to the subject. He thinks that it is time to include sex as one of the cultural arts and not as a biological or even relational urge. Great lovers, he says, have always known that sex was an art as well as an instinct. Art is in fact, one of the great transformers of raw instinctual power. Sexuality appears regularly in the dream state. We may find our dream egos in all sorts of sexual postures with either sex. This is not something to be afraid of, he observes, but something to enjoy and come to terms with if the dream behaviour appears negative. On one level, sexuality is the urge for unity with a split part of oneself. On another level, sexuality and its image state in dreams expresses our relation or lack of relation to the life force—how warm, how vital, how alive am I? Or, on the other hand, how inhibited, cold and afraid am I to express my basic animal nature?

In Sufism, a woman's body and her sexuality are a part of the sacred substance of the earth. Part of the fascination of the feminine is that she embraces the wonder of creation—the beauty of God's feminine form. When the anima is projected on to a woman, there is a sense of both completion and awe. The beauty of the inner and outer are fused together. Her sexuality and the earth are inter-related as in the following dream, related by Llewellyn Vaughan-Lee (1992), the Sufi writer, where the dreamer realizes the preciousness of the earth and is led into his lover's body, initiating him into the sacred mystery of the feminine:

> Half-naked, I meet Aurelia, a former girlfriend of mine. Suddenly, I am aware that she too is half-naked. She is wearing a tunic, open at the sides so that I can see her marvellous modelled body. Her muscles are strong; she reminds me of Diana.
>
> We start playfully to try and catch each other and within a moment we are out in nature. We run across a

freshly ploughed field of rich brown soil. The ground curves up to a small hill, and Aurelia is nearly ten meters away from me, lying stretched out on her back on the bare ground.

Half flying, I jump towards her, landing very softly on her belly so that I directly touch her vulva. Suddenly, I realize that her belly and the area between her legs is covered with crumbled earth. I put my hands into the soil, feeling how precious the earth is. Then, as in a holy ceremony, Aurelia takes me very softly and leads me into her body.

Past Life Dreams

Many people, especially in India, believe that they had lives before the present one. We often have dreams which reflect our past lives but since we do not live in awareness, our minds constantly occupied with thoughts, we miss reality even in the waking state. In sleep, when we are even less aware, we cannot recognize a past-life dream. Our present behaviour, according to past-life theorists, is based on what we have been doing for several lives and therefore, we are bound to have dreams of the past. We review old films, as it were. If we look at the dreams of past lives, we could recognize patterns that have persisted, and this could trigger change. Here are two instances that are interesting and intriguing.

Grandma Visits

A young manager who worked in the industrial relations department of a large corporation shared this dream during a dream workshop:

> What I remember is that I am in a room which is very old. I would say the time frame was 1920 or so, (much before I was born) because there is an old style radio and old wooden furniture in the room. There is a lot of activity on the street, people going around. I suppose it is the time of the Indian freedom movement or something like that because all the men are wearing white kurta and pajama and khadi caps. My grandmother is in the room discussing something very important with my father. I clearly remember seeing my grandmother, even though in real life I have never seen her or even seen a photograph of her's ... but throughout the dream there is a lot of movement and there is tension in the atmosphere ...

When the dreamer worked on the interpretation of his dream, it appeared to relate to the industrial relations conflict that was going on in his company at that time. However, the dreamer insisted that though his feelings of anxiety and powerlessness related to his present situation, the images in his dream suggested that he had gone through the same feelings in a previous life. Minor disturbances involving groups of people created a great deal of anxiety for him, even though he was not involved in what was going on. There was nothing that had occurred during his childhood or in his family that could explain his behaviour.

Soldier in Hot Pursuit

A more dramatic experience occurred during an international dream group workshop. A young German woman shared a long dream with the group, where she was being chased by an unknown figure. In the dream, she runs through the town, across a bridge, even takes a ferry to try and hide on a nearby island, but the person chasing her continues to be in hot pursuit.

The dreamer was asked to close her eyes, return to the dream, stop running and turn around to face her pursuer. It was difficult, she was afraid, but she finally did it and realized that the person chasing her was her husband. Somehow, that realization did not close the issue for her, so she had to go back to the dream to discover that this time, she was being pursued by her father. The dreamer then underwent a catharsis and spoke at great length about her relationship with her father and how he had persecuted her over several years even after she left home. 'He was continuously after me,' she said.

Somehow, I had the strange feeling that the dream work

was not yet over. The dreamer was softly persuaded to go back to the dream again. She broke out into a cold sweat, began to breathe heavily, and finally, after several tense minutes, spoke in a whisper, 'I am being chased by a soldier who is carrying a sword. It seems to be in the ancient times because he is wearing some kind of an armour. I think I am a soldier too. And we were both in a battle.' I suggested to the dreamer to try and confront her pursuer, which she did.

After a little while, her breathing returned to normal, she became very quiet, and finally, opened her eyes. She said:

'Now I can understand an incident that happened to me last month. I went to Dresden, where I am planning to move house shortly. I had never been to the city before. As I was strolling along the sidewalk near the centre of town, I noticed a large monument which was dedicated to the Unknown Soldier, or something. I was strangely drawn towards the monument. I crossed the street and went towards it. As I came closer, strange feelings overwhelmed me and I could hear the sounds of battle-horses neighing, swords clashing, people crying out in anger and pain. I could not believe what was going on. I looked back across the street where I had come from, and everything seemed normal. The traffic was moving and nobody seemed to notice me or what I was going through. I am quite sure I must have been there during the battle.'

Colourpuncture and Dreams

Peter Mandel, the German medical scientist, whose basic work is the therapeutic use of colours on the body, discovered specific zones or centres on the human body which correspond to the three primary colours. These zones are located along the spine, from the bottom to the top. He was amazed to discover that there was the possibility of being able to influence not only psychological tendencies with the help of colours, but also that rays of coloured light are capable of healing acute or chronic illnesses. His concept, called 'Colourpuncture' is now becoming popular in Europe as an alternative healing process.

Colour therapy fulfills two requirements in a unique manner: first, it is gentle and painless, with no side-effects; and second, it has a positive effect on the cells of the body.

Peter Mandel believes that physiologically, the skin is capable of registering pressure, touch, vibration, temperature and pain because the skin is the gateway to the inside of the body. Throughout all ages and cultures, the skin has been the medium for treatment in most illnesses. The Chinese, especially (whose tradition spans centuries) make use of the skin as a medium of treatment, especially through acupuncture.

According to Peter Mandel, when certain zones along the leg are stimulated by coloured light and the esogetic oil which he manufactures, specific dreams are evoked. There are altogether eight zones. The following are the kind of dreams that would be evoked through colourpuncture:

Zone	Colour	Category
I	Green	Dreams of elimination and secretion: dreams of letting go.
II	Red	Dreams relating to bodily/physical reality; dreams relating to existential questions—'Who am I', 'where do I stand in my life'.
III & IV	Orange	Dreams dealing with human relationships.
V	Violet	Dreams relating to events that go back into childhood; pre-natal events; events from past lives.
VII	Violet	Dreams relating to higher levels of consciousness, for example, lucid dreams, breakthrough dreams.
VIII	Turquoise	Dreams that are very stimulating, relating to action and growth.

Note : The missing number VI indicates that no dreams are elicited from that zone and therefore, no colour is ascribed to it.

The Indian Association for the Study of Dreams undertook an experiment in September 1992 to validate Mandel's hypothesis (Jethmalani, 1993). While some interesting patterns emerged, for example, there were common elements in the dreams of the experimental group (elements, characters, settings), it was not possible to arrive at any definitive conclusion. However, among some dreamers, problems that had been suppressed for years surfaced, such as the death of a parent or early childhood incidents. Needless to say, these findings have no bearing on the efficacy or otherwise, of colourpuncture.

6

Corporate Dreams

In the winter of 1983, I designed and conducted the first dream workshop for corporate executives at a leading management training centre in Pune, India. At that time, I was director of the centre, and responsible for both its academic and administrative functions. For a decade after this first dream workshop, it continued to be an annual event.

Despite initial resistance, these 'Creativity and Dream Workshops' were so popular that dreamwork was often included in other Human Resource Development (HRD) programmes. Sometimes, corporations held in-house workshops on creativity and dreams. Dreamwork was also used in an organization development effort, to change the culture of a large R&D centre. The objective of the effort was to enable a stagnating group of scientists to become vibrant and highly motivated. Much of this work has been documented, and has been presented as papers at international seminars in the United States, Europe and India. The seminars were variously sponsored by the European Foundation for Management Development, the International

Association for the Study of Dreams, the Tata Institute for Fundamental Research and the Max Mueller Bhavan.

Since its inception, hundreds of managers all over India have attended these dream workshops. Unlike in the West, where managers are chary about discussing their dreams thanks to Freudian psychoanalysis, in India there is a kind of refreshing innocence among most managers; an openness, or a readiness to share their innermost problems, which often borders on naiveté. At in-house workshops, however, the culture of the corporation determines the extent to which managers are willing to share their dreams with their colleagues. Public sector managers, whose careers and promotions are fairly well-defined, feel more comfortable at such workshops, as do managers of companies where organizational politics and intrigues are minimum. It is important to add that with globalization and increased competitiveness, trust among colleagues is taking a beating in Indian organizations.

Corporate dreams can be divided into two categories. The first is related to personal lives and revolve around family and similar relationships. The second is associated to problems related to work. Generally speaking, the following are the issues that recur in managerial dreams:

- Power and powerlessness
- Autocratic bosses

- Women managers and the glass ceiling
- Corporate vision
- Job insecurity
- Second home

Dreams of Power and Powerlessness

The corporation is a political arena where power plays an intrinsic part. Power is probably the most important variable in an organization. It can be thought of as the organization's energy. Power in itself, is neither good nor bad. It is natural and inevitable. It can be used effectively to obtain positive and lasting rewards for people and corporations, or it can be misused to hurt people and corporate interests. Enron being one recent example of how power should not be used!

Managerial dreams are often born out of these power dynamics. They tell about heady highs or depressive lows or, now in increasing numbers, of people who are lingering in-between. Here are some examples which will give you a taste of what really goes on in the executive unconscious.

Stuck in the Muck

The first is a dream of a middle-aged project manager:

> I am rowing a boat on a river. It's a beautiful day, and everything around is lush and green. Maybe I am somewhere in Africa. I feel very happy and full of life. As I

move on, the river narrows and begins to grow shallow. I can see a tiny village in the distance, but there don't seem to be people in the village. My boat slows down. It is getting caught in the slush below, and however hard I try to row I find that I'm stuck.

Interpretation

This dream very clearly describes the manager's behaviour and his ultimate dilemma. He becomes enthusiastic about a new project each time however, (indicated by the lush green) as it nears completion, he loses the will and the energy and gets stuck—till another project comes up. Working on his dream, the manager realized that his failure was connected to his lack of faith in his colleagues, subordinates and people in general. The first reaction to the dream is, 'Where are the people?' The dreamer manager wanted to do everything himself, without involving other people in his project—indicated by the village (his goal) with no people in it. This realization motivated him to make concerted efforts to interact more with people and to involve them in his projects.

Dreams also urge us to get out of rut and to grow into the greater fullness of our potential. It is best portrayed by the following dream:

The Flying Snake

The new, volatile environment in which executives have to

operate often overwhelms them and renders them powerless. This feeling of powerlessness often surfaces in their dreams. The following is a dream of an oil company executive who was sent to Assam, India, on a new assignment:

> I, all of a sudden, went home. It was in a village, the original native place where I was born, with a dense jungle around and I found that things were not in proper order. The jungle was not the same that I knew as a child. Then, suddenly, I saw a very big snake and surprisingly, it was black and very, very long. It was flying over the trees. It was falling on the trees. It was peeping at us. It was not trying to disturb us but was trying to pose itself. At times, it went inside the house. I was in great panic. Then I went to my mother. I asked her about it. My mother said, 'Don't kill that snake. It is very good. It is going to protect you. Have you looked at it?' I said, 'Yes, I saw it.' She said, 'It should not be stared at. It is like a God. Don't bother, nothing will happen to you.' Then I went into the jungle, and got some solace.

Interpretation

The dreamer had been transferred by his corporation to his home state in Assam. The local tribe in his part of the state were demanding a separate state, which they called Bodoland. Some members of the movement had become militant and used guns to further their cause. The dreamer had come back to his village home after a long spell and was surprised to find the place in turmoil. One day, a group of militants, all young boys, asked him for the loan of his official jeep for an assignment. He refused. The dream is a fallout of his refusal. It deals with his constant fear that he was now being watched (which was true) and his anticipation of harm. In this typically Indian dream, the mother figure steps in to assure him that being a Bodo himself, the militants would protect him, not harm him. She warns him not to be too inquisitive about their activities. The mother converts a scary snake into a protective deity! Meanwhile, the dream helps him to cope with his fears, which is one of the important functions of dreams.

Boss Blues

Traditionally, there have been five types of corporate powers—coercive-status, reward, knowledge and information and the power derived from charisma and people-orientation. There is a great deal of writing about new types of power through globalization, technology and the emergence of flat organizations, especially in Information Technology companies, where power is based on the individual's knowledge and merit. In these new organizations, the relationship with the organization is contractual and not based on hierarchy and position. Unfortunately, the new values are still to emerge in most organizations and managers continue to face bosses who exhibit traditional behaviour and, as one research study showed, refuse to 'respect them as persons'. Here is a dream of a senior manager who, harassed during the day, continues to see his boss at night—as a mad elephant:

> I was walking along a street when I saw an elephant, white in colour, with uplifted trunk. The elephant was running, thumping its feet on the ground with great force, as if it was angry or mad, and I felt it was chasing me. I was sure it was following me. I quickly sat in a rickshaw (a three-wheeler taxi) and asked the man to drive off as quickly as possible. Finally, I reached a place where I knew some people. I told them, 'I would like to hide myself as I am being followed by a mad elephant.' They ask me to come in. They had a house made of glass. Even the walls were made of glass. I stayed for a while in the house. They offered me food, and I don't know how much time I spent with them. After some time, I raised the curtain and peeped out to see if the elephant was still around waiting for me or not. But there was no elephant, so I came out. There was nobody around. I made sure there was no danger. Then I came home. I feel that I came home, but that is not clear to me.

Interpretation

The dreamer had no difficulty identifying the elephant as his overpowering boss. He identified the man in the glass house as a senior colleague who helped him, but was himself vulnerable, since the boss was so powerful in the corporation.

Dreams of Women Managers

There are many issues that are reflected in the dreams of women managers such as the conflict between home and career. There are also issues of sexual bias and harassment. For successful women managers, the glass ceiling is often a cause for frustration. This seems to be a global phenomenon, despite the success of women CEOs, exemplified by Fiona Carla of Hewlett Packard.

The woman manager in India is still struggling to find her place. Societal and family attitudes towards working women make the critical difference. Read this moving dream of a finance manager who, just when she was beginning to enjoy the fruits of her success, had to face sudden opposition from a powerful male superior:

The Bull Dozer

> I climb three steps. I am standing on top of the steps wearing a beige colour sari and a pink coloured shawl looking very beautiful, poised and confident and I am looking up at the sky. I can see the bright blue sky through a tree. It is a very big tree with bright, deep green leaves. I have a smile on my face looking up at the sky. I find, in front of the steps, there is sand—a lot of sand. I then see a lot of

people. I cannot see their faces properly, but I can see some wearing blue shirts, some wearing white shirts and others in pastel shades. They were standing behind me, down the steps in a semi-circle. They are all looking up at me with smiles on their faces and full of admiration. There is no exchange of words or sound, but the thing is that I am laughing and fully confident and happy. I feel that they are also very happy about it.

I suddenly see a bull coming very slowly through the sand, approaching straight towards me, and I am still feeling confident and happy and looking at the bull. Then I see the people are still looking at me, but now they have become a little stiff. Then the bull comes closer and closer and then starts pushing me. I can feel the pressure and I feel very suffocated. I feel that my head, everything, the entire body is covered, only my eyes are open. I could still see the bright sky and deep green leaves and then my eyes fall on Joydeep. He raises his head but does not say anything but I feel he is saying, 'Chandama push it sideways, push it sideways.' And I know that I have to do that, but I find it so difficult, but then again with great effort, I try to push the bull's head sideways up to my shoulder, and the dream breaks.

Interpretation

The dreamer had little difficulty in translating the metaphors and feelings in the dream to interpret what was going on in her waking life. The only daughter of Bengali parents, she was one of the first women in Kolkata to become a chartered accountant, a much sought after professional qualification. Encouraged by her family, she rose in her career ('I climb three steps...') and had a number of male subordinates and colleagues who appreciated her. However, at the time of the dream, a senior manager felt threatened by her competence and her career advancement. He tries to 'bull doze' his way into her work arena, and as the dream reveals, is successfully, if temporarily, thwarted. Joydeep is a male friend and colleague, whom she turns for help, but afraid of the bull himself, he only provides lip service. 'How like a man!' was the reaction of the dream group.

Driving over My Flowerbeds

Now contrast this Indian dream with that of a British woman executive who is bothered by sexual advances in her new workplace, and is nostalgic for the old company she worked for. The cultural differences are quite sharp, but the problem is the same:

> I was in my flat in London where I lived 10 years ago. It was a little, shabby basement flat. I was in my back room. It was sort of half underground. I suddenly see the smiling face of a lorry driver, who is sitting in a lorry which is standing by my window. It is as close as it can come and he grins in a leering sort of way. I storm outside and say, 'What the fuck

are you doing? How come you are driving all over my flower beds and everything?' Down the slope near my window it is winter, everything is covered in snow, everything is white, which it never is in winter. There is another man with the lorry driver. They take a look at me, and I can see a road going down. They were driving down the road. I am satisfied that my anger has some reason, that they could have done some damage. I imagine they could have destroyed some flowers by going over them, and then I return to the flat and realize that I have forgotten the key, but the door is open anyway and I can get in and I now see the room. It is sort of shabby, old walls, big fur rug on the bed. I feel very nostalgic about it because actually I have a new room that I was to take over and I don't want to lose this one and I am sad that I might have to give up this old and shabby room.

Interpretation

The English woman saw her dream as expressing her anger against the male intrusion of her privacy, destroying the delicate and aesthetic parts of herself. She also saw in the dream, her conflict between giving up her old life and entering a new one. The winter scene, suddenly made her realize that she was no longer young and that she was now at an older stage of her life. The feelings in the dream appeared to suggest a movement from a more secure to a less secure existence.

Dreaming the Corporate Vision

Most vision statements are based on data from the past and perceptions of the future. The end product often turns out to be a numbers game, ensuring that the future is simply the modified past. Corporations, especially those in the new technology areas, are trying to break through this unimaginative process of envisioning the future. In an era of continuous change, the future is unpredictable and a vision set in stone has little meaning or relevance. The other important need is to involve top managers in contributing to the process of developing the vision statement. Dreamwork is the ideal means by which top management can achieve creative, breakthrough thinking of developing a vision by dreaming together.

A few companies have let us experiment with vision dreaming for their organizations. Those who have gone through the process were amazed at the efficacy of this radical approach. The process requires senior managers to attend a workshop where they literally dream together to develop a vision for the corporation. The method has several advantages. In the first place, the top manager is freed from the shackles of playing the traditional numbers game and the conditioning of the past because the dream performs that function. Second, when senior managers share their dream for the corporation with their colleagues, it brings in an emotional dimension to the process of developing a vision. Third, the fact that the management incubate the vision together can bring the collective consciousness into play. This assures a deeper level of commitment by the group to the Vision Statement.

How The Vision Workshop Works

The design for the vision workshop is simple. Members of top management meet in the evening prior to the workshop (without the CEO) and discuss the long-range outlook for the company. They use the brainstorming method to generate alternatives, so that they will be able to look at a large number of ideas—from the very conservative to the very radical. In the next step, the managers work, reflect, and even meditate on what should be the future of their corporation. Finally, they lie down, relax and hope for a dream in the night. The lights are put off to deepen the relaxation, and the managers are instructed to focus on the corporate future.

The next morning, the senior managers meet and share their dreams. It is surprising how many new insights, creative ideas, perceptions and original, futuristic thoughts and images emerge from a night's dreaming! At the next stage, the group prepares a collective collage of their corporate dream. They use pictures from old magazines, colour crayons or even grass, moss or rocks picked up from the garden, for a three-dimensional collage. They work together on the collage, explaining to each other the reasons for their inputs. The atmosphere is not serious. It should be a playful, creative exercise. After some initial hesitation, the managers loosen up and begin to enjoy themselves.

When the participants are ready with the collage, the CEO is invited to join the group. He is presented with the collage which represents the hopes, aspirations, and dreams of his senior managers in relation to the future of the company. This can be an emotional session. The collage forms the basis for the ensuing discussion of the vision statement of the corporation.

Here are two examples of dreams from a vision workshop:

Floating on Waves of Music

> I found myself very light like a feather. I start floating over tunes of music. However, instead of going up and up and up in the sky over musical waves, I was going down, into the great valleys and deeper. It was very scenic, the valleys, and unfathomable. I started gliding down over waves of music till I reached the bottom of the valley where I found all sorts of fish going around and, to my surprise, coils. Various coils like the ones we manufacture, stacked in different ways, and fish going around them. Beautiful, colourful fish. Then I stared critically. I noticed that those coils were made of gold.

The second example:

Dream Run

'Still in my unconscious state, I desired a dream about my organization.' The dream unfolded in the following way:

> The factory is illuminated with colourful bulbs. There was light everywhere. Then I go into the room, inside the factory. I find no one, it is like a vacuum. I wonder, why there is nobody around or inside the factory. There comes a voice from something, from an unknown place saying, 'It is a holiday.' Then I ask, 'If it is a holiday, why are all the lights on?' The voice says, 'It is a trial run, the illumination. It is for a show to be presented tomorrow. We are working to see what the lights look like.' I say, 'Okay, great!'

The images and content in both these dreams suggest bright futures for the companies. In both dreams, there is a high emotional content that encourages the feeling of togetherness, which is very important in a vision exercise.

Job Insecurity

With globalization and the increasingly high levels of competition, corporations have resorted to Voluntary Retirement Schemes (VRS), leaner organizations, outsourcing and so on, which have affected layers of middle management.

All over the world, older managers are either jobless or work under stress, fearful of losing their jobs at any moment. The world seems to be heading for a great crisis, threatening the health and lives of thousands of corporate managers. These stressful times are reflected in corporate dreams.

Here is a typical dream of a senior manager, Jamshed Mody, who sees himself as having worked loyally for his company for several years and having contributed greatly towards its success. The culture of the corporation has now changed and it has adopted new values. The company is not as direct and open with its employees as it used to be. So although Jamshed continues to be an employee, indirect hints and subtle statements make him insecure about his job. This is Jamshed's dream:

The Scary Elevator

> I am speaking on the telephone to one of the flat owners of my Society building. I am the Secretary of the Society. The flat owner is reprimanding me for not looking after the interests of the Society especially the lift (elevator) which is malfunctioning. Next, I am around the building checking whether everything is in order. I tell myself this building is not the one in which I actually reside. As I am standing there, an elevator comes down and my sister comes out and tells me very curtly not to use this

elevator and to use the one which is at the rear of the building meant for the servants. I was not even aware that there was one more elevator. All of a sudden, I see myself with my nephews and nieces and my younger brother standing on the ground floor for the lift. Now the elevator has come down and we all get in. All of a sudden I see myself on the topmost floor. I am tied to a chair with a seat belt kind of contraption and so is a child next to me. Next to the child is my younger brother also seated with a belt. There is a big chasm in the floor of the elevator and all the remaining children are on the other side of the chasm. Everyone else there seems to be at ease with the situation except me. I look down and see the shaft of the elevator. My legs are dangling. I don't know how I will get down and exit the elevator. I panic. The others are laughing and joking. They are encouraging me to be brave and try and get down. I refuse. I tell them please give me some time to think and I will come up with a solution. I am helpless and begin to cry as I think there is no solution. The children are talking and joking among themselves. After some time I see that there is the gate of the elevator right next to me. A thought occurs to me that if that gate can be opened then I can easily get out of this jam. I ask the children if anybody can help me open that gate. They say it is very simple. One of them jumps across to this side of the chasm with a flat piece of metal and opens the door. I very carefully undo my seat belt and get out and feel myself

> standing on the landing outside. I am relieved. So much so that I begin to cry, but hold myself from breaking down. Then my mother comes along and asks me to come in. I don't recognize the house. I tell my mom that I have lived in this flat for almost 20 years and I have not seen this part of the house. Then I come into the other room which is familiar territory.

Interpretation

This is a powerful dream that speaks for itself. The dreamer finds he is no longer acceptable to his own colleagues (family), in a company where he had spent 20 years. He finds that even the workplace has changed beyond recognition. The children represent the new, younger employees who are quite at home in the changed organization. The dreamer identified the mother with a sympathetic senior colleague.

A Second Home

Many managers are married to their jobs. Often they are workaholics who have forgotten that there is a life outside the organization. Increasingly, the company does not recognize their devotion. Yet, it still fulfils both the ego and social needs of the manager at the workplace, so that he does not have to look elsewhere. Some corporate dreams depict the workplace as a second home for the manager.

The Office Picnic

This phenomenon is brought home poignantly by the dream of a senior woman bank manager, who was in the hospital undergoing treatment for cancer. The manager dreams that she is at a bank staff picnic. At the picnic, she finds the nurturance that she is seeking, but the dream is also precognitive and forewarned her of her impending death:

> I am at Urlikanchan, in a lovely grassy meadow. Our bank staff is having a picnic. It's a lovely happy atmosphere. I feel constrained, because I have not brought any picnic lunch with me. The girls are very kind and friendly to me. As if reading my mind, they say, 'Madam, don't worry, we have brought lunch for you.' There are small tables laid out on the meadow, covered with checked cloth. There are no chairs. The boys are dressed in gaudy silk, like acrobats. I am enjoying it all. Everyone there is from the staff of the bank. I know some of them. Some I don't know. I suddenly remember that a job had not been completed. I go to a phone booth and make a call and I am satisfied that the job has been done. I spot Farida, an old friend. She looked exactly as she did before she fell ill and died of cancer. Except that there was some froth of blood at one side of her mouth. She smiles a small smile and looks at me sadly. I smile and talk to her. She is trying to tell me something, but I don't know what it is.

Shortly after this dream, the manager passed away. It appeared that towards the end of her life, she preferred to return, in her dreams, to where she felt most secure and happy—her workplace, the bank.

7

Phantoms of the Night

Nightmares are dreams that produce unpleasant feelings in the dreamer and cause high levels of anxiety. They usually occur late at night, often during the last three hours of sleep. According to Dr Ernest Hartmann (1973), Professor of Psychiatry, nightmares often appear in a long REM period of 20-30 minutes. Due to the nature of the dream, it has been observed that the dreamer has high blood pressure, or an increased rate of heart beats. Sometimes, nightmares can even appear to the dreamer as soon as he falls off to sleep. These are called hypnogogic nightmares.

Children often have nightmares during a certain period of their development, and these may come and go at different times. Adults usually experience nightmares when they are going through periods of intense stress. It is unusual for an adult to experience nightmares regularly. When this happens, it is probably because the adult is trying to come to terms with a frightening event, memory or is anticipating disaster in the future.

Ordinarily, what people call nightmares are severe anxiety dreams, which result in the dreamer waking up suddenly in fright. Apparently, the content and feelings in the dream are such that they cannot be contained within the limits of sleep, so the dreamer awakes. More severe nightmares, in which one feels caught up in uncontrollable terrifying experiences, such as the nightmares experienced even now, by Vietnam veterans, occur during the non-dreaming phase of sleep. When woken up, the dreamer does not remember much of the dream content. Dreamers who experience such nightmares generally need psychiatric help.

The nightmare can often be a reflection of an unconscious pattern of relationships and conflicts in a family. The family may be going through a normal period of stress, such as school exams. Or the family may experience habitual drunkenness or violence which could cause unusual and chronic stress in the family, leading to children experiencing nightmares, though this is not always the case.

The Scary Black Fiat

Here is an example of a recurrent nightmare from one of my dream groups. The dreamer was a young woman in her early thirties:

> It is night time. I am running on a road. There are trees along both sides of the road. I am alone. There is a black

> Fiat car following me. I cannot see who is driving it. I keep running and running and it keeps following me. I don't remember whether it hits me or not, but I wake up in a cold sweat.

Nightmares occur because what is not faced consciously in the waking state, is brought to the forefront of the mind forcefully during sleep and this creates fear or perceived danger of annihilation. To deal with nightmares, one should evoke healing symbols and guides and face the dream situations resolving them instead of waking up. Situations that create anxiety must also be dealt with. Anxiety is fear without an object. To deal with anxiety, identify real objects for all your fears. Use such concrete fears as motivations to change the destructive into the constructive.

For example, during my corporate career, I was once reluctantly involved as a mediator between the management and the union of an organization. At one stage I seemed unable to please either side, and both appeared to be upset with me. This is when I had a nightmare:

Sudden Flood

> I was swimming in the river near Panaji, the capital city of Goa. I was aware that close by, the river joined the sea. It was a pleasant morning, and I was feeling happy. As I swam, I noticed, to my right, in the middle of the river, a cosy-

looking cove. I get out of the water and into the cove, where I lie comfortably, watching the river flow quietly, and the city of Panaji nearby. Suddenly, I noticed that the river was rising. It seemed as if both the sea and the river, from opposite sides, were flooding the cove menacingly. I began to panic. I knew my life was in great danger. Just this thought made me alert in the dream itself. I became lucid. Instantly, I conjured up a submarine-like boat. It was a strange contraption, but it took me to the shore where I was safe.

Factors which Cause Nightmares

Studies show that one-half of all adults have experienced nightmares at some time or the other (Gackenbach and Bosveld, 1989). A survey of 300 US college students in 1989 revealed that almost three-fourths of them had nightmares at least once a month. Nightmares can be caused by several factors, including unnecessary and heavy homework for children, which plague countries like India and Japan, change of residence, strained relationships, illnesses, especially high fever and traumatic experiences. Sometimes such events in childhood can cause recurring nightmares into adulthood. Those who experienced the earthquakes in Latur and Gujarat are reported to still have nightmares about the events in their sleep. When people have gone through terrifying experiences, they continue to fear that the experience will be repeated.

Thus nightmares represent the fulfilment of their worst fears brought to life in great and realistic detail. Some writers suggest that whatever horrors you personally believe to be the worst thing that could happen to you, are the most likely subject of your nightmares.

However, people's understanding of why nightmares take place differs from culture to culture. In some cultures, nightmares are seen as the true experiences of the soul wandering in another world as the body slept. Other cultures see nightmares as a visitation of demons. In fact, the word 'nightmare' originates from medieval English denoting a female evil spirit thought to lie upon and suffocate sleepers, plus the old English 'mare' which referred to an incubus, who was a demon who came in the night to steal sexual pleasures from sleeping women.

Medical scientists have discovered that some drugs and medication cause an increase in nightmares. Drugs (and alcohol) suppress dream or REM sleep for a few hours till the effect wears off. Then there is a sudden burst of dream energy just before you wake up and such dreams can be nightmarish in character.

Calvin Hall (1966), one of the earliest of dream researchers takes an interesting view of nightmares. He looks at the fact that gratification of impulses does not always proceed smoothly. Obstacles are encountered and detours are necessary. The principle obstacle is the dreamer's own conscience—a network of conceptions, of right and wrong, of sanctions and prohibitions. That is why many dreams are unpleasant, even terrifying as in the case of nightmares. The dreamer is being chased by a man with the knife, a burglar is entering his room, a lion is about to spring on him, the house is on fire, he is drowning or he is arrested and put in prison. These are all punishment dreams, says Hall. Why is the dreamer being punished? Because he has violated one of the commandments of his conscience. He has rebelled against authority, or he has gratified a forbidden wish, or he has committed a misdeed. The nightmare is the price he pays for doing something wrong. Such dreams provide us with information about the dreamer's conceptions of the penalties which will be inflicted upon him should he disregard his conscience and yield to temptation.

Nightmares might recur in childhood, but the same themes may also haunt us well into adulthood. As a person matures and faces more of his fears, he may resolve the problem in the dream in the waking state. The key issue is to come to terms with the root fear. It is not easy to pull the root out and let it dry and die in the sunlight. So, often the nightmare may change both in terms of its content including the dream figures, but it will persist even in adulthood, till we come to terms with the root fear. As children, we may have a recurring dream about being chased by a wild animal. As we get older, the energy of the wild animal (violence, unrestrained lust, brute force) may modify and integrate through life's experiences, and emerge later in a less primitive form in dreams. Instead of a wild animal the energy may appear in the form of a bully or a lusting man or woman. If we can confront and work with this powerful figure it may then transform itself again, into perhaps an aggressive boss or partner.

Freud's View

Nightmares, according to Freud (1976), were the results of masochistic wish-fulfilment. Freud's basic conviction was that every dream represented the fulfilment of a wish. 'I do not know why the dream should not be as varied as thought during the waking state,' Freud wrote, 'In one case it would be a fulfilled wish, in another a realized fear, or again a reflection persisting into sleep, an intention, or a piece of creative thought...' It does not appear to reflect reality. So according to Freud, the victims of nightmares, must have a strong waking desire to be humiliated, chased, violated, or tortured, which is fulfilled in their scary dreams.

Stephen LaBerge (1985), who has contributed a great deal to our understanding of lucid dreaming, believes that the anxiety experienced in nightmares is an indication of the failure of the dream process to function effectively. Anxiety arises, he says, when we encounter a fear—provoking a situation against which our habitual patterns of behaviour are useless. If a person experiences a recurring anxiety dream, what he or she obviously needs is a new approach for coping with the situation, represented by the dream. However, it is obvious that a nightmare has arisen because the dreamer was unable or reluctant to face the dream content or the dream figures in waking life. This leads to unresolved conflict which surfaces in the unconscious in the shape of a nightmare.

LaBerge recommends lucid dreaming as an exceedingly powerful tool for coping with anxiety dreams or nightmares. In our wakeful state, we function under the assumption of boundaries. When we become lucid, we often continue to work under these boundaries till the full impact of the illusion of boundaries strikes us. While lucid, we dissolve all boundaries and move into higher states of consciousness. Here, it appears that there are certain kinds of people who suffer from nightmares. According to Ernest Hartmann, leading research psychiatrist and nightmare expert, people who tend to have 'thin' psychological boundaries are prone to frequent nightmares. They are clearly sensitive people in many ways—easily hurt, empathic—and some can be unusually bothered by bright lights or loud noise. In their interpersonal relationships also, these people have thin boundaries, where they can enter into relationships quickly and trustingly. They can even have thin boundaries about their sexuality. They do not see themselves as totally masculine or totally feminine. They are bisexual in their actions or in their fantasies. Even in their dreams, they have thin boundaries and can easily move from one dream to another. Their sleep-wake boundaries are also not very solid. Often, they are not certain of being awake for some time in the morning, especially if they have had a vivid dream. Lucid dreams are discussed later, along with other methods of dealing with nightmares in detail. The next section discusses night terrors and how they are different from nightmares.

Night Terrors

Sometimes, people experience what is called a night terror. It is different from both nightmares, as well as the regular night dream. Though it also occurs during sleep, it is devoid of symbols and images. The person just awakens with a sense of overwhelming terror, awe and unearthliness. Night terrors can be accompanied by sweating, convulsive body movements and even screams. On the other hand, nightmares are usually peopled by unusual events, powerful, frightening situations, or a combination of both. Often, the dreamer suddenly awakens with a huge sense of fear or anxiety.

People who have night terrors are often misdiagnosed. The most common one is a simple nightmare. Any of you who have had a night terror can say with certainty that they are not even close! Another common misdiagnosis (especially among veterans) is Post Traumatic Stress Disorder (PTSD). For this reason a description of the difference between nightmares and night terrors has been included.

The symptoms of night terrors generally include sudden awakening from sleep, persistent fear or terror that occurs at night, screaming, sweating, confusion, rapid heart rate, inability to explain what happened, usually no recall of 'bad dreams' or nightmares, or a vague sense of frightening images. Many people see spiders, snakes, animals or people in the room, are unable to fully awaken, difficult to comfort and with no memory of the event on awakening the next day.

Night Terror or Nightmare?

Nightmares occur during the dream phase of sleep known as REM sleep. Most people enter the REM stage of sleep around 90 minutes after going to sleep. The circumstances of the nightmare will frighten the sleeper, who will usually wake up with a vivid memory of a long movie-like dream. Night terrors, on the other hand, occur during a phase of deep non-REM sleep, usually within an hour after the subject goes to bed. This is also known as stage four. During a night terror, which may last anywhere from five to twenty minutes, the person is still asleep, although the sleeper's eyes may be open.

When the subjects do wake up, they usually have no recollection of the episode other than a sense of fear. This, however, is not always the case. Quite a few people can remember portions of the night terror, and some remember the whole episode.

Although night terrors can occur at any time during a person's life span, the most common is reported in children between the ages of three and five. More recent studies however, report that many adults, as well as children as young as six months, experience night terrors on a weekly basis. Night terrors usually occur fifteen minutes to one hour after going to sleep. The longer the person is in NREM (the stages before REM) before the night terror begins, the more afraid he will be when it occurs. Keep in mind though that not everyone falls asleep at the same time as others. This requires a sleep study to determine what stage of sleep you are in when these events occur.

Night terrors have been shown to appear in stage four of sleep. This is what separates them from nightmares, which can occur at anytime during sleep. It is possible to make a night terror occur in some people, simply by touching or awakening them during stage four of sleep. Why night terrors occur is still a mystery. The mind is supposed to be practically void during the deeper stages of sleep. The subject will awaken gasping, moaning and crying, or screaming. Breathing rapidly, they will sit up in bed with a wide-eyed terror-filled stare. This panic will often last anywhere from five to twenty minutes. Research has found the most amazing aspect of night terrors is that it generates a heart rate of 160 to 170 beats per minute. This is much faster than the normal heart rate that can be attained under the most stressful circumstances.

Some things that can help bring out a night terror are stress, certain medications, being over-tired or eating a heavy meal before going to bed. Many different medical ailments contribute to the frequency of night terrors. While these factors do not cause night terrors, they just seem to put your body into the state where a night terror can manifest itself.

There seems to be a common thread in how night terrors manifest themselves. Many people who remember a night terror have talked about seeing animals or people. Quite a few people see snakes and spiders. At first it appeared that people were only seeing things that they were afraid of during waking hours. After more research it was found that only a small percentage of people were afraid of what they saw (in night terrors) during waking hours. Some people remember the night terror. Some do not. There is no explanation as to why some have no recall of the events during a night terror.

It has been found that the best method of controlling someone during a night terror is to hug and reassure them and tell them that everything is all right. Agree with what they are saying and doing. Sometimes it is not possible to hug them. Do not try to force physical contact. Do not shout at them or tell them they are only dreaming, as this seems to only upset them even more. The method seems to work better in children than in adults. The most important thing to remember is that a person having a night terror does not know what he is doing. Make sure that there are no objects nearby that they can hurt themselves or others with. It is perfectly safe to wake someone who has a night terror, though you must remember to be gentle!

It is also interesting to note that two other disorders, sleepwalking and bed-wetting, are experienced during stage four of sleep. Even more interesting is the fact that all three of these sleep disorders often run in families. Some families will dismiss night terrors as nightmares and blame the problem on television or other bedtime stimulus. Episodic night terrors do not signify psychological problems. However, do not tell the subject that nothing happened. It is allright to tell that person, the next morning, that he had a night terror.

Strategies for Coping with Nightmares

The first strategy to deal with nightmares is to understand its nature. Kaplan-Williams describes nightmares as adversarial dreams—any dream that makes us wake ourselves up out of fear. In these dreams, we are typically opposed and attacked. These attacks create fear in the dreamer who runs away or ultimately escapes from the situation by waking up. Running away may be a temporary experience, yet, it excludes half of life. So the first major step, in effectively dealing with adversarial forces in nightmares, is not by fleeing but by coping with them directly. It is better to stay present in an adversity than to have it destroy us through our flight.

A second strategy is followed by the American Senoi Dreamwork tradition. Dreamers are trained to stop running and to start relating in the dreams. Their belief is that when we flee from something, we give it our energy in addition to its own, thereby making it more powerful. If, however, we turn and face our enemy, the enemy might turn into a friend. We are most afraid of what we have not yet integrated within ourselves.

The third strategy is to understand the nature of fear. You must be clear that fear is itself the perception of possible loss. We are constantly beset with worry, of losing our spouses, of children deserting us, of the loss of life before our time, of failure in our endeavours, of loss of property or money and the loss of job. None of these is actually happening. But, such events in life do happen to others, and sometimes to ourselves. Yet, our experience of fear is of possible, and not actual loss. We fear the possible, not the actual. We fear something in the future, which may never arrive. This understanding makes it easier for us to cope with fear.

The fourth strategy is based on the Gestalt approach of Fritz Perls, discussed earlier. Fritz believed that dreams are simply projections of parts of ourselves which we are unwilling to own. 'Every part of the dream is you.' Through Gestalt dreamwork, the dreamer learns to conduct a dialogue with the various characters in the dream till he comes to the realization that each character is really part of himself, which he has projected into the dream. For example: the angry man or the sensual woman are really your projections. By accepting your anger or your sensuality, these parts integrate with your personality and lead to greater wholeness. You realize that what you feared in your nightmares was nothing but parts of your own self which you had disowned.

In Gestalt dreamwork, the steps to deal with nightmares are as follows:

1. Choose a dream and decide which characters or symbols you want to isolate. Choose the interesting characters in your dream or odd objects or even faceless individuals. Allocate them spaces or chairs within the room and give them names.
2. Do not choose too many characters. Keep things simple and start with two or three until you get used to the process.

3. Set out an extra chair for you to sit in as a witness or observer. Use this space from time to time as a place from which to assess the progress of the interaction and also to record the events that occur.
4. As you carry on the dialogue with the characters and then become each one by turn, solutions and resolutions will emerge as the energy of the characters evolves and transforms.
5. Feelings can be confronted, new approaches and insights may emerge, and a healing process and a sense of clarification will usually be effected. You may experience a catharsis, which will accelerate the process. This is not unusual.

The fifth strategy is active imagination, first introduced by Carl Jung. It enables the dreamer to elicit information by becoming an active participant in the dream process rather than being a passive observer. While dreaming we feel we are organically part of the flow of sensations and feelings, but this experience soon fades as we move into the waking state. This strategy suggests that we can go back to the dream state if we wish and make any changes that did not feel good or right during the dream.

You can work with the active imagination strategy on your own. Find a quiet room and relax in a chair or lie down on the ground, but stay alert. Try and elicit information from the key characters in the dream. Try out an alternate course of action. Be creative. Generate alternatives even if some of them seem absurd at the moment. Listen to your inner wisdom, and trust the dream process to unfold in a new way. When it begins to happen on its own, just absorb it.

The sixth strategy is guided imagery. For this technique you will need someone who is sensitive and aware, and who will act as your guide. Here is an example from one of my recent workshops. The marketing manager of a large automobile company told us about his recurring nightmare:

The Trekker who Flew

'Before I narrate the dream I must give you some background. I am a member of a trekking club. Every weekend we take to the hills. A few months ago, we discovered a steep cliff from where we got a simply gorgeous view of the sunset. One of our group fell in love with the place and the scene. He was literally enchanted. He said, "This is so beautiful. I would like to jump off the cliff and die." A few weeks later, that is exactly what he did. Ever since then I have this recurring nightmare:

> I see myself in three roles. The First Me is lying on my bed in my room and watching the other two. The Second Me is running towards the edge of the cliff with a determined look on his face. The Third Me is sitting at the edge of the cliff watching the Second Me running. He runs, attempts to

> fly and falls right down into the valley with a thud. The Third Me looks towards the First Me on the bed and says, 'It's all over.' I get up with a start, my heart pounding and body bathed in sweat.

I decided to use guided imagery to help him get rid of his recurring nightmare. First, I asked the dreamer to close his eyes, and to try and get in touch with the images and feelings in the dream, as if it was happening right then. I asked him to breathe deeply and gently and then said, 'I am your guide. You are watching your dream from your bed. The Second Me is getting ready to start his run. This time he takes no chances. He gives himself a really long start. You can barely see him in the distance. His arms are less inhibited. He is able to move them out a bit, at first, then slowly he extends them fully. He is now able to flap them like wings as he gathers speed. You can see him feeling exhilarated, he is about to take off ...' Before I knew it, the dreamer shouted in excitement, 'I'm flying! I'm flying!' Fortunately, he came back, slowly opened his eyes and looked around. 'I flew right up to Kanya Kumari, the tip of India', he declared, 'I could see all the green fields and towns and rivers below'. During the next session, which was dream art, he had painted the cliff and a person with beautiful, large colourful wings. He looked at me and said, 'The other two persons have disappeared.' And they had.

One must be careful when using this method. You

must only help the dreamer to finish his unfinished business, to meet his need or desire. Never project your own ideas into it.

The seventh strategy is to look at the characteristics of nightmares and then to develop tactics to cope with them. Patricia Garfield (1991) says that following a physical or emotional crisis, the nightmares that follow are of two types: being chased or attacked, or other terrifying events. In both these dilemmas, the dreamer usually feels afraid or helpless, or has little or no control, or gets hurt, and dies.

The first tactic she suggests is to change your behaviour in the dream itself: face your dream enemies. Say to yourself in the dream, 'I don't have to run and hide. I can turn around and face my dream enemy.' Or order the pursuer to stop, 'You're only a dream image!' Sometimes merely confronting the villains in your dreams is enough to deprive them of their power. Take action. Tigers sometimes shrink into pussycats. The second tactic Garfield suggests is to fight the dream enemy. If confronting the enemy does not work, then you can fight them. You can even call for help from allies or draw upon inner resources. The third tactic is to reconcile with your dream enemies. If combating a part of yourself in dreams troubles you, then you can approach your enemies in a spirit of reconciliation. You can ask your dream figures for advice or gifts to remember them by. The fourth tactic is to love them.

Stephen LaBerge (1985) reported a breakthrough when he was able to tell a horrific giant that he loved it, incorporating the dream image within himself during the dream.

The eighth strategy is lucid dreaming, which is an approach to becoming conscious during your nightmare. This technique can be learned and practised quite easily. To turn lucid in your dream, George Gurdjieff, the Russian mystic who lived and worked in Paris, suggested that you should go through the day repeating an action. For example, you might raise your hand. Every time you remember that you have to be lucid in your dream, raise your hand. Then at night, when you see a raised hand you remember, 'Hey! I'm dreaming!' The second way of becoming lucid is to make a resolve, either through the day or just before going to sleep, after rotating your consciousness, as described in the chapter on incubation. The third, is to ask your guru or your God for help, just before you fall asleep. A fourth method, is to ask yourself during the day, 'Am I dreaming or not?' If you do so often enough, you will realize you are dreaming. In a way, all the techniques are simply variations of the theme. All of them can help you become lucid during a dream.

The point is, what do you do when you are lucid? As some therapists have suggested, you can confront or fight your dream enemies. Others have suggested that you can befriend, even love them, and integrate them in your personality. All of them have strongly advised against killing these dream figures.

The Eastern strategy, which existential psycho-therapists like Eric Craig have supported, is not to interfere with the natural phenomenon because it can become 'a narcissistic flight from one's fuller possibilities'. This approach involves simply observing what is happening, aware that you are involved, but that it is only a dream. The last step, which is difficult, is to simply remain a witness, where there is no involvement at all.

8

The Healing Power of Dreams

Tread softly, for you are now on sacred ground. Your journey into the dreamworld has brought you to mysterious springs within the self that heal sick bodies and stressed minds. A perennial source of energy that flows through your inner space and keeps you healthy. For it is dreams that warn you of an impending illness when your health is at risk. They can direct you to see your physician when you are beset by physical or psychological illness, and they can provide the support you might need to cope and become healthy again. Sometimes, they suggest treatment which your doctors were unaware of. The healing power of dreams is truly immense.

Since ancient times, in Egypt, a sick or disturbed person would sleep in the temple, after swallowing a potion to foster dreaming. In the morning, the temple priest would interpret the dream and administer the cure prescribed by it. Later, the Greeks began to focus on dreams and the problems of healing.

They used dreams for diagnosis and cure of chronic physical complaints often associated with sterility. A similar practice was also prevalent in India, where barren women spent the night in the temple praying for a dream that would help them to conceive. Aristotle came to the conclusion that dreams might be used by physicians as an indicator of an ailment or malfunctioning that had not yet manifested itself in outward signs. Hippocrates, the founder of modern medicine, had studied dream symbols and concluded that they were very important tools in the diagnosis of an illness, especially as early warning signals.

It was Hippocrates (Garfield, 1991) too, who refuted the notion then prevalent, that illness was a punishment from the Gods. He said, 'Every disease has its own nature and arises from external causes, from cold, from the sun, from changing winds.' He advised against meddlesome interference, saying, 'Our natures are physicians of our disease.' His ideas of using 'similars' to cure illness was in a way, based on the Greek mythological idea that only that which hurts can heal. In the case of Achilles, who had an arrow shot into his heel, the rust from the arrow was used to heal his wound. This idea is fundamental to the practice of homeopathy: like cures like. Homeopathy widely uses dreams, because it believes that dreams are one of nature's miracles, not the result of a wandering mind.

An important contribution has been made by Dr Farokh Master, a leading homeopath in India, in his compilation of a *Homeopathy Dictionary of Dreams*. According to Dr Master, a dream can be an expression of what is happening in the physical body, a way of balancing physiological and psychological activities in us, and an enormous source of insight and information about the dreamer, which can be used by the physician.

Dr Master's work is the result of 20 years of experience studying dreams and dream processes in his patients. Based on the dreams, he has suggested homeopathic medicines for each disease.

Today, contemporary medicine is taking a serious look at dreams. Medical journals publish articles on subjects such as, 'The use of dreams in the initial interview.' The Journal *Dreaming* features articles such as, 'An explanation of the parallels between Freud's 1895 Irma Dream and his 1923 cancer' and 'The prevalence of nightmares among patients with asthma and chronic obstructive airways diseases.'

How to Use Dreams for Healing

For the common reader, the best and most practical way to use dreams for healing is to scan the dream for indicative images. Very often, the body is represented in the dream as a car, truck, house or building. Remember the first rule in dream interpretation: look at images only in relation to yourself. Is the dream talking about your body? Does it match with what is going on in your life at the moment? What is happening to the car or truck? A broken-down car, an aging building, a defective truck or object may suggest illness. Dreamers often picture the disorder in their bodies as mechanical problems in their cars. Which part of the car is defective or needs attention? The wheels might suggest the legs or feet, the carburetor, an internal organ. The engine might suggest the heart. However, you must not jump to conclusions, as the feelings in the dream will indicate how authentic the problem is.

You might, for instance, dream that you are running on a low fuel tank or on reserve, which might indicate that your energy is low at that time. A full tank might mean the opposite—that you are full of beans! Cars appear often in managers' dreams, and they often relate to power or lack of it. The questions that will reveal the meaning of the dream could be: are you at the wheel, in charge, or have you been relegated to the back seat? Is the car without brakes—have you suddenly lost control, or is the body out of control, perhaps not responding to medicines. These dreams help, because they may be obvious pointers, but like most people, you may live in blissful unawareness in the waking state. Or, you may not be willing to confront the issue.

Ernest Rossi (1988) is a clinician and hypnotist in Los Angeles, who has worked extensively with the connection between the mind and body. He says that researchers have identified a three-stage process, whereby the mind influences the cells:

1. When we think, or imagine a picture or feel an emotion, the frontal part of the cerebral cortex generates nervous impulses.
2. These emotions are filtered through the emotional areas of the limbic hypothalamic system.
3. The nervous impulses are then converted into chemical impulses called neurotransmitters, or messenger molecules.

This is an important finding, because it reinforces the belief that understanding your dreams will give you clues about what is happening in the body. Consequently, influencing your dreams through the process of Incubation can help in the healing process.

Patricia Garfield's Questionnaire

Patricia Garfield (1991), who has written extensively on dreams and healing, has suggested a simple, practical and useful way to interpret your healing dream. Answer the following questions with regard to your car which is in trouble (it might also be a truck, bus, airplane or ship) and the answers will reveal the message of the dream:

The One in Charge:

1. Who is at the steering wheel?
2. If not yourself, what is this person like (spoiled, reckless, crazy, trustworthy)?
3. Where are you sitting (driver's seat, passenger front seat, passenger back seat, floor)?
4. Who are the other passengers, if any?

Interpretation

Whoever is at the wheel will indicate the aspect of yourself which is in control. Your location in the car will indicate how you assess your position. Are the other passengers helpful, supportive, threatening, or stressful?

5. What is the condition of the vehicle? What is its make, colour, size and state of repair? Is it big and difficult to handle? Is it small and crammed or small and flexible?
6. How is it functioning? Are the brakes working? Is it going too fast or too slow? Do internal parts break down? Do you have enough fuel?

Interpretation

Answers to these questions often relate to feelings you have about your physical body or the way you are currently moving through life. Going too fast or being unable to use the brakes suggests you are pushing yourself too hard. Going too slow would indicate inadequate energy. A breakdown suggests body impairment or difficulty in some relationship.

Road conditions:

7. What is the condition of the road? Is it muddy, icy, slippery, full of ruts, uphill or downhill, is it an expressway, a super highway or a village lane?
8. What are the other conditions of the environment? Are you on the ground, in the air, in the water? Is it snowing or raining? Are there obstacles blocking your path?

Interpretation

The answers to these questions would suggest the feelings you will have about the conditions and obstacles. Ice and snow often indicate feelings of treacherous, slippery or tricky situations. Mud usually relates to messy conditions. Ruts, obstacles and uphill driving indicate strenuous conditions. An expressway could mean easy going to some dreamers and dangerous conditions to other dreamers. Check with yourself, how it feels like in the situation you are facing right now.

Direction:

9. Is there a direction, purpose or a goal to your trip? Are you on track? Stuck in the rut? Missed a turn?
10. How do you feel about the journey?

Interpretation

Answers to these questions relate to your present purpose. Getting off track or being stuck in a rut suggest difficulties in achieving your present goal. Missing a turn could indicate a missed opportunity. Please remember that even if the road is difficult, you may still arrive at your destination. If you are happy making the journey your goal is worthwhile: if your journey is burdensome, the dream may be depicting a distasteful duty.

Work on the answers to these questions, assuming that the car in the dream (or whatever other vehicle it is) represents your physical body moving through life at the moment. What do the answers tell you about the current condition of the body, or the way in which you are living your life. This method of elaborate questioning can be used with almost any other kind of dream and will reveal what the message of the unconscious is for you.

Let's take an example. A middle-aged man had the following dream:

The Faulty Leak

> I am in an old Air Force hangar where an old type Avro aircraft is parked. Apparently, Indian Airlines is not able to fly its passengers, so the Air Force has reluctantly agreed to carry them in one of their old aircraft. The Avro

is wheeled out of the hangar and a pilot or mechanic has climbed on to the top of the plane to check it. He discovers a leak, raises an alarm and everybody scrambles for cover expecting the plane to blow up. I fall flat on the hangar floor and urge a fellow passenger to do the same. However, it turns out to be a false alarm. The Avro soon takes off.

Interpretation

The dreamer had suffered two heart failures and had a slight leak (a thin rim of pericardial effusion) in the heart which was not curable. This condition had made him anxious, since he feared it would suddenly create a crisis someday. During the evening prior to the dream, the man began to experience an uneasy feeling in his chest. He called his doctor, who advised him to immediately see his cardiologist. The dreamer however, procrastinated. The day following the dream, however, he met his cardiologist who told him that it was a false alarm and the uneasiness was probably caused by flatulence!

The dreamer faced two options in his dream; Indian Airlines, which was the legitimate carrier and an old Air Force plane which was a standby arrangement, exactly like the choice he had of the two doctors. The leaking plane clearly indicated his physical condition (a leak in the heart). The false alarm in the dream also coincided with the 'false alarm' in his physical condition. The dream served both as a warning as well as a reassurance to the dreamer that all was well. This dream message helped the dreamer to deal with his anxiety and stress. Physiologically, after he met his cardiologist, his heart rate normalized, his breathing became easy and the muscles relaxed.

Recurring Dreams and Healing

Who will Marry Me?'

Recurring dreams can also keep knocking at the door till the dreamer confronts an issue and takes action for her physical well-being. Here is the case of Anita, who was 35 years old, married with a young child. For two years Anita kept having the same dream:

> I am sitting at the edge of my bed feeling depressed and lonely, and asking myself, 'Who will marry me? Who will marry me?'
>
> She used to get up with a start holding her stomach tightly. Anita noticed that the dream came during her menstrual cycle, which was severe and lasted several days. This irregularity affected her sex life and consequently threatened her marriage. After working on the dream with a friend, she sought medical help. The doctors suggested that she should have a hysterectomy, something she had unconsciously feared and was unwilling to confront. The

operation was successful, and it changed her relationship with her husband. After the operation, the dream all but disappeared, resurrecting only once, when she was in Japan. But this time she knew she was married and had a child!

Three Dreams of Cancer Patients

Dreams have tremendously powerful ways of working, especially in the case of serious illnesses like cancer. It is unfortunate that the medical fraternity who are not directly involved in cancer treatment seem, by and large, mortally scared of the big C, and even refuse to mention the disease by name. There is just not enough communication between cancer specialists and doctors of other disciplines. Dreams on cancer make a strong plea for integrating different streams of medicine, so that a more holistic treatment is available to the patient. Here are three cases:

A Prayer Answered

Parveen Major was a handsome woman in her thirties who lived an independent life and held a senior position in a bank. She was also a dream enthusiast and was the treasurer of the Indian Association for the Study of Dreams for a few years. Parveen believed her keen interest in dreams was a great help, both at work as well as later, during her illness. Parveen was diagnosed as having cancer of the vertebral column. As a result, she could not walk at all, both her legs were paralysed. During this time, Parveen had a series of dreams that followed the deteriorating state of her health. The doctors had told her that she would never be able to walk again without crutches. One evening, before she fell asleep, she used the incubation ritual, where she imagined herself to be dancing, moving, walking, running, and returning to normal—to be able to walk and work again. That night she had the following dream:

> I am in a medium size, bright, white, empty room. It has a large window covered with barbed wire but through it, I can see the blue sky, and that the sun is shining. Inside the room, an old lady is lying on the bed with a two year old child next to her. There is no other furniture in the room. I am hopping and jumping around the room, happy to see the sun. I spy a wooden picture of Zarathrusta on the wall in a beautiful frame. I go up to it, rest my forehead on the bottom of the frame and say, 'Thank you God for making me well again.'

A week later, Parveen walked through the hospital doors without crutches and with little support. And she was back home!

Message from a Dead Father

In 1997, I was diagnosed with cancer (Non-Hodgkin's lymphoma). I had to undergo treatment for nine months, which included chemotherapy and radiation. My oncologist had drawn up a programme for eight cycles of chemotherapy treatment. In the early stages of the chemotherapy, my dreams were in colour, but as the poisons invaded my body and brain, my dreams were in dull, depressing black and grey. After the seventh cycle, I had the following dream:

> I am sitting on a large, red leather suitcase which I remember, belonged to my father when I was a very small child. I am in a simple, bare room by the sea-side, and I am sitting against the wall near a corner. There is an ordinary bed in the room. My deceased father gets up from the bed and looks at me and asks, 'How are you?' I reply, 'I am fine.' He looks at me doubtfully, slowly shakes his head and walks out. I look at the trunk that I am sitting on. It is full of old mud and moss, as if it were a long buried coffin.

I was quite disturbed by the dream and saw it as a clear warning message from my dead father. Next day, I cancelled the eighth and last round of chemotherapy. Apparently, as my oncologist confirmed later, I had already been given too much Farmarubicin, one of the chemotherapy drugs, which could damage my heart. Despite cutting down on the chemotherapy, I still had a left ventricular failure. Had I undergone the eighth round of chemotherapy, I would have most likely joined my father.

The Lake of Life

Messages from dreams are often very powerful and seem to originate from the Source itself. They are beyond human understanding. The following dream depicts how awesome but compassionate God, or the Source, is:

Fredrick D'Silva was my colleague in the Tata Corporation, and we often worked closely. He had a zest for life and lived it to the fullest. When he was still in his thirties, Fredrick was diagnosed as having cancer. He suffered a great deal, since most of his internal organs had been removed. One day he sent me a message asking that I should see him. It sounded urgent. I remember it was a few days before Christmas. As I entered his room in the hospital, I noticed his face was filled with joy. The moment he saw me, he said, 'I had a dream. They are sending me home for Christmas.'

This was hard to believe, because the doctors outside his room had just told me there was no hope left for his recovery. But the patient was full of his dream and keen to tell me about it.

This was Fredrick's dream which he recounted to me from his hospital bed:

> I am walking along a pool where there are many people who are happy, moving, enjoying, some in couples. I am covered with a blanket, and feeling cold and shivering. As I try to move forward, I fall and I am unable to get

> up. Suddenly, I feel two strong arms lift me up and throw me into the lake. The person also jumps into the lake besides me and shouts, 'Come, swim with me, this is the lake of living water. Follow me and have nothing to fear.'

Fredrick came home on 23 December, in time to celebrate Christmas with his family. Friends, to this day, remember how happy and joyful he was. In the early hours of 28 December, Fredrick passed away. As the dream had revealed to him, he was being taken from the confines of the world to eternal life.

Signs to Watch for in Healing Dreams

Dreams not only warn of impending illness and help diagnose problems, they also keep changing over time to assure the dreamer that he is well on the way to recovery. Dreams for example, change from black and white to colour. Dream experts suggest that you should keep a dream journal by all means where you can record all your dreams. Keep a Dream Journal by all means, but record only important dreams or dreams during illness or an emotional crisis. It is during these periods that you could have a series of dreams, all connected and leading to some kind of definite conclusion or final solution to your problem.

Dream signs of improving health:

When our health begins to improve, our dreams forecast or express these positive changes by different imagery:

1. New growth in plants or newborn animals appear.
2. Protection from images that have endangered us.
3. Flexibility occurs in formally stiff images.
4. New clothing reflecting the new body image.
5. Healing takes place within the dream.

Nearly all physical illnesses have a psychological basis, as therapists have realized over the last century. We are actually in the process of rediscovery, because as we have seen, the ancients had no difficulty with this concept. They understood that there is a basic energy that moves freely through us when we are in a healthy state, but that this energy can be blocked if we are stressed or unhappy in some way and may then manifest as illness or disease. It was accepted that this special energy pervaded the body and had a life of its own that could also express itself in a dream. Eastern cultures, therefore, value the dream as a mirror of the activities of this energy, which is released from its physical vehicle during sleep.

9

Creative Problem-Solving Through Dreams

As we learn more about our dreams, we begin to see glimpses of the richness and possibilities of our potential self—that part of our personality that has remained hidden, and that we now find difficult to recognize. As you continue to work with your dreams, you will begin to discover these new possibilities; to discover treasures that you only need to reclaim. You discover your true creative nature. And this should hardly be surprising, because since the beginning of time, human beings have sought to give creative expression to their thoughts and feelings.

In the primitive dwellings of Europe, India, Egypt, and the near East, there is fascinating proof of man's earliest attempts to express himself. Since the time of the Cro-Magnon man, our ancestors have been painting amazing images of bison and unicorns on the walls of the caves in which they lived. It is these artistic creations, found deep within the caves of Lascaux, that distinguished Man from his animal forebears, and have had a remarkable effect on human development.

Creative dreams too, have a lineage older than recorded history. Artists and mystics have always used their dreams for spiritual and creative inspiration. Dreaming itself is proof of man's creativity. It provides access to the subjective world through which we can explore and understand our innermost self. Every night, the most unimaginative of people go to bed and begin to paint in exotic and vivid colours, a multitude of images and scenes which require immense imagination. The dream itself is a remarkably creative and inventive occurrence. Can you imagine that millions of dreamers go to sleep nightly and each produces dreams which are unique? It also appears that this great creative work is effortless. We transform mundane experiences into beautiful visual displays, interwoven with myriad feelings. It is the one resource that is enjoyed equally by the king in his palace, and the beggar sleeping under a tree.

Whatever one might believe about oneself, the truth is that everyone is creative. Every night we produce carefully crafted plays, and even musicals. Sometimes we produce a comedy or a farce. At other times, tragedies and soaps. The problem arises when we awake, and seem to forget the endless resources of creativity we drew upon in our sleep. Awake, we live mostly, boring, mundane lives. And we lose touch with our creativity—a multifaceted phenomenon—which could have helped us bring into the world new, innovative and unconventional ideas or products. Many creative dreamers believe that every moment of your life is infinitely creative and the Universe is endlessly bountiful. Just put forth a clear enough request, and everything your heart desires will come true. All you need to do is to accept the gift when it arrives. And yet, there are those who have accidentally made discoveries, or designed products, in their dreams, but fail to disclose it to others for fear of ridicule! Our culture, it seems, does not still acknowledge the creative power of dreams.

Scientist Dreamers

The story of the German chemist Friedrich A. Kekule (Delaney, 1979) is well known. He had tried for many years to find the molecular structure of the benzene. Then, as he dozed in front of a crackling fire one cold night in 1865, he reported having a dream:

> Again the atoms were juggling before my eyes...my mind's eye, sharpened by repeated sights of a similar kind, could now distinguish larger structures of different forms and in long chains, many of them close together; everything was moving in a snake-like and twisting manner. Suddenly, what was this? One of the snakes got

> hold of its own tail and the whole structure was mockingly twisting in front of my eyes. As if struck by lighting, I awoke...

This dream led Kekule to the realization that the structure of the benzene is a closed carbon ring, a discovery that revolutionized modern chemistry. When he reported it to his colleagues at a scientific convention in 1890, Kekule concluded with the remark 'Let us learn to dream, gentlemen, and then we may perhaps find the truth.'

Howe and the Strange Spears

You may have heard of Elias Howe (Delaney, 1979), who had been attempting to determine where the eye of the needle of a sewing machine should be located. He dreamt that the king gave him 24 hours to complete the machine so it would work, otherwise he would be put to death. He worked and puzzled, and finally gave up. Then he saw himself being led to the place where he was to be executed. As he walked along, he noticed that the warriors all carried spears which were pierced at the head. Instantly, the inventor found the solution to his problem! While he was asking for more time, he awoke. It was 4 o'clock in the morning. He jumped out of bed, ran to his workshop and before 9 o'clock, he had moulded a needle with the eye at the pointed end which helped him complete his sewing machine.

The Periodic Atomic Table

Mendeleev (Delaney, 1979) developed the structure of the periodic atomic table of elements after three days of working on it without sleeping. He then went to sleep and dreamt the perfect solution to the chart. Not only did he dream of the elements that already existed, he also provided two blanks for elements that would be discovered in the future.

Even Einstein...

Einstein traced his theory of relativity to a dreamlike experience he had when he was an adolescent. In this dream, he was reportedly riding on a sled. As he went faster and faster, the stars became distorted. This intuition stayed with him, and after a series of mathematical transformations years later, emerged as the theory of relativity.

And Others: Writers, Painters, Composers, Saints!

Scientists are not the only creative dreamers. William Blake, the English painter, whose work has a haunting, dream-like quality, was greatly influenced by his dreams. If we look into the lives and work of artists like Goya, who produced monsters and nightmarish figures from his dreams, and surrealists like Dali and Ernst, who took actual images from their dreams, the influence of this unconscious phenomena on creativity becomes clear. Even symbolists like Redon and Gauguin used dream imagery in their work. Similarly, Descartes went in and out of sleep to dream parts of his Discourse on Reason.

The Devil's Sonata

There is the lovely story about Giuseppe Tartini (Gackenbach and Bosveld, 1989), the Italian composer, who at the age of 21 dreamt that he had sold his soul to Satan. In the dream he handed his fiddle to the devil:

> But how great was my astonishment when I heard him play with consummate skill a sonata of such exquisite beauty as surpassed the boldest flights of my imagination. I felt enraptured, transported, enchanted; my breath was taken away, and I awoke. Seizing my violin I tried to retain the sounds I had heard. But it was in vain. The piece I then composed, the Devil's Sonata, was the best I ever wrote, but how far below the one I had heard in my dream!

The Swedish playwright, August Strinberg said he believed in dreams because, 'my brain works sharpest when I'm asleep' (Delaney, 1979). Ingmar Bergman credits his dreams with some parts of his movies. The influence seems clear in *Wild Strawberries*. Robert Louis Stevenson (1892) said the ideas for his book *The Strange Case of Dr. Jekyll and Mr. Hyde* came from a dream—which is not difficult to believe. The range of creative dreamers is so wide and varied, even an anthropologist, Hermann Hilprecht, had an astounding dream that helped him decipher the original inscription on a votive cylinder. Mahatma Gandhi, the apostle of peace and non-violence, writes that the idea of *satyagraha* (non-violent resistance) came to him in a dream.

How Paradise was Found

In his book about the life of the poet Dante, Boccaccio narrates how, after Dante's death, several concluding cantos of the Paradiso could not be found. The poet's sons looked in every possible place without success. Finally, convinced that they would not be able to find it, the sons decided to write the cantos themselves. Jacopo, one of the sons, had a dream which caused them to discontinue the efforts. Jacopo dreamt that his father, Dante, led him to his old bedroom in another house where his death had taken place. Pointing to one of the walls, he said, 'What you have sought for so much, is here.' On waking up, Jacopo, accompanied by family and friends, hurried to the house to which he had been led in the dream. Attached to one wall was a hanging frame. Looking closer, they found a niche in the wall. And in it, the thirteen cantos required to complete Dante's composition.

Creativity and the Universal Mind

Creative dreams seem to draw on facts and information from beyond the individual mind; from what has been called the

Universal Mind. A striking instance is given by the widow of Louis Agassiz (Gackenbach, 1989), who tells of her husband's breakthrough achieved in a dream which drew from sources outside his knowledge: 'He was trying to decipher the somewhat obscure impression of a fossil fish on the stone slab where it was preserved. Weary and perplexed, he put his work aside and tried to dismiss it from his mind. A few days later, he awoke from a dream where he had seen his fish with all the missing features perfectly restored.' He then went early to the Jardin de Plantes, thinking he would see something that would put him on track, but nothing did. Again, he saw the fish in his dream that night and again he failed to decipher its features. The third night, the fish reappeared in his dream, vaguely at first, but at last with such distinctness, that he no longer had any doubts towards its characteristics. Still half-dreaming, and in perfect darkness, he traced its features on a sheet of paper he had kept at his bedside.

In the morning he was surprised to see in his nocturnal sketch features, which he thought it was impossible the fossil itself would reveal. He hastened to the Jardin des Plantes, and with his drawing as a guide, succeeded in chiselling away the surface of the stone under which portions of the fish proved to be hidden. When wholly exposed, the fossil corresponded with his dream and his drawing, and he succeeded in classifying it with ease.

In his book, *Across the Plains*, Robert Louis Stevenson has a chapter on dreams, in which he describes his own experiences. By making a suggestion to his unconscious mind, just before falling asleep, he was able to experience vivid dreams which he used extensively in his literary work. Stevenson credits most of his writing to 'the little people who manage man's internal theatre'. He recognized that unconscious activity surfaced while he was asleep.

A greater and deeper understanding of the source of dreams comes from the famous poet Bettinelli (Delaney, 1979), who said, 'The happy moment for the poet may be called a dream, dreamed in the presence of the intellect, which stands by and gazes with amazement and open eyes at the performance.' The source is vaster than the intellect. But what is the source? Some writers have suggested that essentially, it can be looked at in two ways:

The first is explained by Dr Elmer Gates who refined and perfected over 200 patents which other inventors had started but had failed to complete. He was able to add the missing ingredient that made the difference between failure and success. He says:

The sources of all ideas are —

1. Knowledge stored in the unconscious mind.
2. Knowledge accumulated by others through the same media, which may be conveyed by telepathy.

3. The great universal storehouse of Infinite Intelligence, in which is stored all knowledge and all facts, and which may be contacted through the subconscious part of the mind.

The second was expressed by Rabindranath Tagore, the Indian poet and mystic, when he answered questions at an interview about his poetry and his creative method:

'I believe that all of us have two beings within themselves. One of these is quite above the other in intelligence and feeling. This is the unconscious self. The other being, the conscious self, is quite a stupid fellow. If this stupid conscious self gets the ascendancy, nothing is accomplished. But if we can only take this stupid conscious fellow and hold him in subjection, and not let him interfere with our unconscious self, then we can reach heights seemingly unattainable.'

Creativity Defined

If one chose to go by the best definitions of creativity, all dreams would meet the criteria by their very nature. Arthur Koestler (1959) defines creativity as 'an act of liberation. The defeat of habit by originality.' This, of course, is what every dream does, if you would only care to interpret it. Rollo May goes further. He describes creativity as the process of bringing something new into birth, and the most basic manifestation of man's fulfilling his own being in the world. A third definition is provided by Zaleznick who says that the creative act breaks out of traditional modes of thinking and sees the world in new ways.

The unconscious mind has been described as a great storehouse of life. Within its structure is found a memory picture of every thought, action and emotion that we have experienced during our lifetime. In the East it would be extended to several lifetimes. It would go back to the time we were dinosaurs. We still carry the original reptilian brain which reacts to any situation only by fight or flight.

Blocks to Creativity

In the waking state, people are much less creative because of the psychological blocks that they encounter. These blocks include:

— A fear of failure
— A reluctance to take risks
— An inability to tolerate ambiguity
— A preference for judging ideas
— An inability to relax
— A lack of access to imagination

In the dream state, as you struggle with issues for which you are seeking solutions, these blocks tend to melt away, or completely disappear. Right from our childhood, we learn to suppress our feelings, creating a rich fantasy world in dreams.

Where do these blocks come from? And why are we not just as creative in the waking state? The most obvious answer is the way we are conditioned and educated. There seems to be a tremendous bias towards logic and certainty in favour of the more ambiguous imagination and feelings. It was Karen Horney (1964) who spoke of the 'tyranny of don'ts' that a child had to suffer. By the time she is six, she is already burdened with a mountain of don'ts on her head – 'Don't cry', 'don't show your anger', 'don't sulk' and even strangely, 'don't laugh too much today because tomorrow you will cry'! Everything possible seems to be done to discourage the expression of feelings. At night, as you relax into sleep, these inhibiting factors loosen their hold over you; the censorship is also suspended. And you are free to participate in your creative world.

The Right and Left Brain Functions

It is generally accepted that the two hemispheres of the brain, right and left, are equal in size and have developed over the centuries to perform specialized functions.

The right-brain functions are responsible for abilities connected with the:

— Spatial
— Intuitive
— Artistic
— Dreams
— Metaphors
— Imagination

— Non-verbal
— Emotional
— Musical
— Visual
— Creative
— Sexual
— Spiritual
— Colours
— Images
— Symbols

The left-brain functions include:

— Logical thinking
— Analytical thinking
— Linguistic abilities
— Writing abilities
— Conceptual abilities
— Verbal
— Mathematical
— Linear
— Reading
— Sequential
— Rational

The Complex Brain

Modern neuroscience has suggested that the centre of our consciousness-controlling processes are in the frontal lobes or the pre-frontal division of the brain, which belong to the tertiary zones of the cortex.

The mind is probably one of the most complex systems in the body, and is constantly being studied. Scientists have been able to observe carefully and see how the dream images are produced. These experts say that more information is produced in the dreaming brain than in the wakened state. The brainstem generates signals (PGO waves) with sensory information, the brainstem responds to these signals but is not activated. These images are the sources of dream images. Although a brainstem is not activated, the signals do trigger a system called the Central Motor Pattern Generator, during REM sleep, which causes the sensation of movement during one's dreams. REM periods, as we have discussed, are when the eyes move back and forth underneath the eyelids according to the brain activity in dreaming. Not only is there a complicated process in the production of the dream image, but in addition, the brainstem is producing signals it causes a reaction called Activation Synthesis Hypothesis or ASH, which creates the contents of one's dreams. ASH is the loss of a neurotransmitter that chemically charges the brain to process information differently. These neurotransmitters help creativity in dreams, but are not always used to their full potential. Ninety-five to ninety-nine per cent of dreams are forgotten because the aminergic neurotransmitters are blocked in REM sleep. However, when awakened in the REM state, the transmitters are opened and information is recorded and remembered; thus, creativity during the dream period is utilized.

Dreams and the Creative Process

There are two basic views that have been expressed on dreams and the creative process:

The first is that the creative process is not enhanced by

dreaming, but when one is asleep, the mind is stress-free and therefore able to think; that is the illusion of the mind being more creative. Stress is something that affects everyone almost everyday. When applied to the creative thought process, it is easy to see how it can become a wall that is difficult to scale

Stress may come from several sources, including work, home and school. In deeper and longer periods of REM sleep, stress is slowly released and becomes less of a factor. According to this view of creativity in dreams, stress is simply shown as a cause for suppressing the mind and blocking the creative problem solving ability in the awakened state.

The other view about creativity in dreams, is that the mind is unconsciously opening doors to information that we ignore each day, but unknowingly process. Brain-wave records show that the dreaming brain is more active than the one that is awake. These records seem to prove that when dreaming, the brain has more capacity for greater work in a given time. Data has been recorded during the REM phase of sleep when the brain is apparently at its creative peak.

Creative Dreaming

Many of those active in the dream world, believe that you can become creative by turning lucid and directing your dreams to paint the pictures or write the poems you desire. Patricia Garfield (1991), a leading proponent, writes, 'Most creative workers of the past have hit upon dream inspiration by accident.' She suggests, '...You can use a technique in which you plan the general content of your dreams, but in this case you are seeking a creative product rather than advice or healing.' She believes that you can plan and control your dreams.

Monte Ullman (Ullman and Zimmerman, 1970), on the other hand, is clear that we cannot consciously control our dreams. Since the dream is a natural resource flowing within us, it requires more than conscious intent to influence the flow. There has to be a genuine emotional investment.

Creativity at its highest level would be defined as what occurs when the you, or the ego, is absent. The ego and creativity cannot exist simultaneously. That is why in most of the examples that have been quoted, the scientist or artist just describes himself as the medium or witness to the creative act. As the famous Italian poet Bettinelli, put it: 'The happy moment for the poet may be called a dream, dreamed in the presence of the intellect, which stands by and gazes with open eyes at the performance.' Many great artists and poets have simply declared in awe, 'We don't know where it came from!'

According to Louis Pasteur, his inventions were 90 per cent perspiration and 10 per cent inspiration. In this view of creativity, the individual has explored all avenues and made every possible effort, even to the point of extreme exhaustion. It is then that he relaxes, and the unconscious takes over. He has used logic and sequential thinking and reached the limits of rationality. Letting go, and in a state of relaxation, as in a dream, his mind is free to take an irrational, creative leap. A quantum leap that provides the break-through solution to his problem. This happens on its own.

Scientists are working on computers based on quantum physics. Several prototypes of the quantum computer are already ready in laboratories in the United States (at Alamo) and in Europe. While the present 8-bit digital computer can only exist in one of 256 states at a time, an 8-bit quantum computer can exist in all 256 states simultaneously. The interesting thing about the quantum computer is that it operates in an unpredictable, capricious way. This capriciousness, this unpredictability, is typical of the work in the unconscious.

It is now accepted that the conscious mind is just the emergent apex, the tip of the iceberg, the top level of a vast and sustaining consciousness. It is from this deep area of the mind that every creative idea emerges, for the scientist, author, musician, inventor or entrepreneur. The unconscious selects its own time and situation under which its insights are revealed. Even if you incubate a problem, unless you have worked on it or it is important to your life at that moment, the unconscious may choose to ignore it. It will decide what is important for you. It will have its own priorities.

Colour in Dreams

Calvin Hall (1953) surveyed 3,000 dreams and found that 29 per cent contained some element of colour, while the rest, he concluded, were 'totally colourless'. He thought, on the basis of his findings, that colour in dreams was merely an embellishment, signifying nothing in itself. Fortunately, a few years later researchers used the Aserinsky and Kleitman technique of awakening the subjects during REM periods and then eliciting information on interrupted dreams. The researchers found that colour was reported in 82.7 per cent of the dreams, leading them to conclude that dreaming should be considered a coloured, rather than a black and white phenomenon. Hundreds of conversations with children and unsophisticated dreamers reveal that, without exception, they all see colour in their dreams. Most often they say it is like everyday colour.

Those who recall and report colour in dreams are usually those who pay attention to colour in the waking state. Since we normally are not aware of the colours of objects until our attention is drawn to them, we may not notice them in the dream unless we are specifically asked to remember. However, if the colour has a significance to which the unconscious wishes to draw the attention of the dreamer, then he is more than likely to notice and remember the colour. Nancy Parsifal, (who has researched the subject of colour in dreams), gives the example of suddenly realizing the colours of the three cars that were regularly parked across the street for more than two years, only when she almost backed into one of them! Just because she did not recall the colours, she says, does not mean there was no colour. This phenomenon apparently occurs in dreams. When colours blend in naturally with the dream setting, it is not noticed.

Psychologists have various explanations for colour in dreams. Some believe it can be communicative, affective or depicting higher imaginative, decorative, aesthetic considerations. Others feel that colour always highlights and dramatizes a particular representation. Or that colour in dreams reflects heightened sensitivity to details of the environment or the depth of inner emotional life. In the latter, colour is symbolic of inner processes. In some cases, colour in dreams serve as an early indication of physical disease.

In the dream data collected through my workshops, we found evidence that would support all these views. The important thing to keep in mind is that colours are often specific to the dreamers, though they could also choose culturally accepted colours. For example, saffron was traditionally associated with religion in India, though it has been associated with politics in recent times. On the other hand, a woman associated purple with her father, because that was the colour of his favourite tie.

Here are some more examples:

Red Alarm

A young man dreamt he was travelling in a train which stopped suddenly before a disastrous accident could occur. He looked out of the window to see a bright red light shining into his eyes. He discovered it was warning him that he was about to take a decision which would have disastrous consequences for him.

White Purity

A young woman saw her deceased mother in a dream dressed in her bridal sari. The mother touched and caressed the dreamer's head, gently pouring a luminous, glowing, light like molten glass into the central parting of her hair. She seemed to be performing an Indian ritual that the dreamer experienced as absolution for past misdeeds. It was a release from the guilt she had been carrying for years. The following two nights, her dreams were dominated by the colour white, signifying the cleanliness and purity she now felt. The houses, rooftops, automobiles and the flowers were all white.

Green Phobia

There was also the case of a man who suffered from diabetes. On the advice of friends and relatives, he began to eat a lot of green vegetables, which he did not mind. However, he did not like bitter gourd (*karela*) which was fed to him often. The man was the disciple of a guru who always wore white, while all his followers wore orange or maroon. One night the diabetic saw everything in his dream coloured a sickly green, that permeated everyone and everything at the guru's ashram. It appeared that he had had enough of the colour!

Meanings Ascribed to Colours

There are cultural and even regional differences in what a particular colour could mean. Green, for example, can signify youth, new life, greener pastures or opportunities. Or envy and spite. It is also often associated with Islam. Orange and red are associated with sexual passion and desire, violence, anger or danger. Purple is the colour of suffering and pain, and is associated with the higher levels of the church hierarchy. Blue could stand for peace and tranquility, as depicted by a blue open sky, or a calm sea.

When I was undergoing chemotherapy, I kept a daily record of my dreams. By the fifth cycle, my dreams had stopped being in colour and had started to be in black and white. That is when I got a warning from my father in a dream, which caused me to stop the treatment. Apparently, it was the right decision. So while one can have generalized meanings for different colours, the right approach must be to let the dreamer alone decide what a particular colour in a dream means to him.

10

Dreamless Sleep: The Mystic Experience

Here we are then, at our journeys' end. Or, is it really the beginning? Are we spiritual beings on an earthly journey? Is there a reality beyond the dream? The mystic experience seems to suggest that there is. The last part of our journey is going to be hazardous, so we will have to take it one step at a time.

The east and the west seem to fundamentally differ in their notions, approaches and experience of dreams. As early as 1958, Medard Boss, the existential psychotherapist, wrote that western philosophy and psychology have always concerned themselves by the portion of the total human phenomenon. He believed that if one had to understand the entire truth, it was necessary for all its manifestations to be studied. Western science had basically confined its explorations solely to the waking state of human life, and had been interested only in the phenomenon observable in this state. However, in the total field of man, two other equally valid conditions existed—the states of dreaming and of deep dreamless sleep.

As the illustration below shows, there are four stages of sleep. We move from the waking stage to the dream stage and in the fourth stage, to dreamless sleep. It is this stage of sleep that the mystics have paid the greatest attention to.

NIGHTLY SLEEP CYCLE

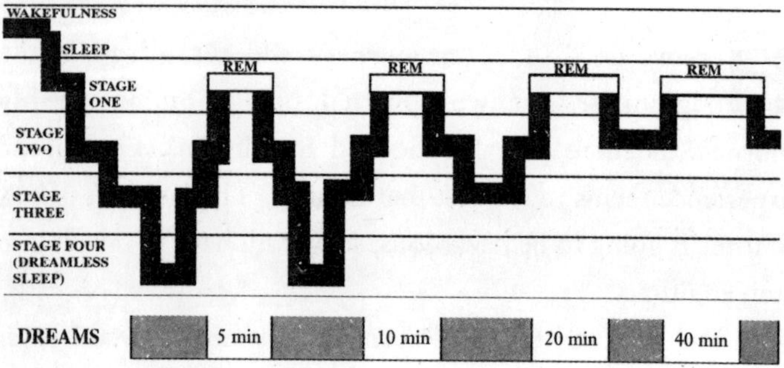

Medard Boss

Medard Boss (1958) acknowledges that in recent times, western psychology has begun to look scientifically at the phenomenon of dreaming. However, he thinks it has not been given the status it deserves. The dreaming person has been judged from the standpoint of the waking state and this way his dream world has been quite unconsciously demoted to a 'something' that is derived from the outside; it has been regarded as its more or less perfect copy, or even as an unreal hallucination. The dreamer's world is just as real to him as the waking world is to a person who is wide awake.

In the east, dreams are taken much more seriously. They are seen as tools of transformation. Moreover, at a certain level of inner work, dreams stop being dreams and instead become spiritual levels of consciousness. Dreams open invisible doors to subtler levels of spiritual growth, awakening in seekers of truth and wisdom, our permanent witness or soul within our conscious selves.

I. Deep Sleep is Made of Happiness Itself: The Mandukya Upanishad

The eastern view of these states of sleep and consciousness were revealed over 2,500 years ago, in the *Upanishads*, which were a statement of condensed philosophical teachings conveyed directly to students from a living master. The *Mandukya Upanishad* specifically discusses the four stages:

Waking *(Jagruti)*,

Dream *(Swapna)*,

Dreamless or deep sleep *(Shusuptid)* and beyond all three,

The Fourth *(Turiya)*.

The waking state comes into play when our bodies wake from sleep and see a world outside. However, according to the *Mandukya Upanishad*, there is something missing here. Our bodies never wake up fully, to a full awareness of what they see. In the waking state, we live in a large universe; but our perceptions of it are partial and inadequate. Through our senses, we only see a few of the many things that the universe contains. Even when we look at a particular object, our senses do not see it properly. They only see an outward appearance, from one of many different points of view. The outward knowing waking state only experiences gross things.

Many things remain unclear and the details are missing. The teaching of the *Upanishad* concludes that, in what we call the waking state, we are not properly awake. We are only superficially awake. That is why we remain unfulfilled and frustrated in our experience of the waking world. To fill this critical gap, and to deal with the frustrations, there arises the need to sleep and dream.

Dreams are the second stage. The dreaming mind, according to the *Upanishad*, is a second aspect of our self-experience. It is described as inward knowing, subtle and burning. In this dream state, perceptions are turned back in. Attention is not diverted a world of objects outside, as in the waking state. Instead, perceptions are imagined, thought and felt within a person's mind. In the dream state, we make finer distinctions and build fuller pictures of the world. Where the gross perceptions of our senses fail, we fill the gaps with subtler faculties of conception in our minds.

In the process of experience in the dream state, our pictures of the world keep getting built, destroyed and built again. This gives us different and changing ways of looking at things and thinking about them. As we learn from experience, old concepts are burned up. In that 'burning', new experiences become illuminated and new conceptions are formed. That is why the dream state and its mental transformations are called *taigasa* or burning energy.

Deep Sleep

This changing process leads to a third aspect of each person's experience which is deep sleep. As the *Mandukya Upanishad* describes it:

> Where one who sleeps does not perceive
> the slightest dream, nor feel desire
> of any kind, that is deep sleep.
> This deep sleep state has come to oneness:
> filled with consciousness alone.
> It is made of happiness itself,
> experiencing that happiness.
> Its gateway is the mouth of mind.
> This is the third aspect:
> of knowing in itself.

While the dreamer might view the deep sleep as blank, dark and empty, the *Mandukya Upanishad* describes it as having come to unity. Deep sleep is seen from its own point of view, as a positive experience in its own right. While we experience deep sleep, it is neither physical nor mental. We experience it as a space where all differences and conflicts are dissolved in bliss. In its own experience it is just bliss, with no difference or conflict to disturb its unity.

Adi Sankaracharya in his commentary on this verse says, 'In deep sleep, the mind is free from the miseries of the efforts made on account of the states of the mind being involved in subject-object relationships. Hence the state of mind in deep sleep is called *Anandamaya*, which means endowed with an abundance of bliss'. However, he points out that this is not bliss itself because it is not infinite bliss. Unlike in the other two states, in deep sleep, consciousness is not differentiated.

Turiya—Beyond the Three

According to the *Mandukya Upanishad*, no passing state can amount to a true awakening. Not the waking state, which gives way to dreaming. Nor the dream state, which dissolves in depth of sleep. Nor even the deep sleep state, whose latent potency gives rise to waking and dream experiences.

To be truly awake, all states must be taken into account. That is only possible from a changeless reality, which stays present in all states. That reality is called '*turiya*' or the 'fourth'. It is called the fourth because it is beyond the three states of waking, dreaming and sleeping.

II. Consciousness is All There is: Ramesh Balsekar

The enlightened ones live in *Turiya*. An example would be Ramesh Balsekar, the enlightened master who resides in Mumbai. According to Balsekar (1992), dreaming is a state of the mind. In deep sleep the sentient being himself is not there. So consciousness in deep sleep, not aware of itself, is the original state. Then in the waking state, the first moment of awakening is the consciousness being aware of itself. Further, if there are other sentient beings, then inter-human relationships arise. However, if there are no other sentient beings, then there is only consciousness observing the manifestation, and there is no sense of 'me'. There is merely a sense of awareness of the manifestation. No 'me' and no 'other' exist.

The question that people ask is, 'How can the waking state be called a dream, when around us we see mountains and rivers which are thousands of years old. How could they be said to have arisen suddenly?' Balsekar's (1992) response is that in the dreams too, this is what precisely happens. There are mountains that are thousands of years old, babies are being born every day, old people dying. You realize the unreality of life only when you wake up from sleep. But then you have simply woken up from your personal dream into this living, waking dream.

Enlightenment, says Ramesh Balsekar, means only one thing: a sudden realization that that which appears real, is really unreal. Then you have the experience of the unreal being real. There is a sudden sense of transcendence, rather a vision of transcendence. That this is all a dream no longer remains a concept. It becomes a reality. The difficulty arises because you think in terms of 'me' being the dreamer of both the personal dream and this living dream. This is not true. Both are the creations of Consciousness. The only dreamer is Consciousness. We are simply the dreamed characters.

What is absent in deep sleep is the sense of 'me'. The identified consciousness is absent, but the impersonal consciousness has to be present. It is consciousness that has been aware during deep sleep but that consciousness is impersonal. The personal identification is missing.

III. The Experience of Pure Being: Ramana Maharishi

Ramana Maharishi (1989) was undoubtedly the greatest sage of the last century. He has often spoken about dreams and sleep. Unlike the others we have discussed, Ramana mentions five states in which the individual abides. To the states of *jagrat*, *swapna*, *sushupti* and *turiya* he adds *turyatita*.

Sushupti, according to Ramana, is a state of deep sleep wherein is experienced the bliss of the Supreme by means of the subtle *avidya* or ignorance. 'Just as a hen after roaming about in the day calls the chicks to her, enfolds them under her wings and goes to rest for the night, so also the subtle individual being, after finishing with the experiences of the *jagrat* and *swapna* for the time being, enters with the impressions gathered during those states into the causal body which is made up of innocence.'

Deep sleep is nothing but the experience of pure being, according to Ramana. The three states go by different names, such as the three regions, the three forts and the three deities. However, the being always abides in the heart. If the heart is not relinquished in the waking state, the mental activities are still and Brahman alone is contemplated. This is the state of *turiya* and when the individual is merged in the Supreme it is called *turyatita*. The vegetable kingdom is always in *sushupti*. The animals have both *swapna* and *sushupti*. The Gods (celestials) are always in *jagrat*; man has all the three states: but the clear-sighted yogi abides only in *turiya* and the highest yogi remains in *turyatita* alone.

According to Ramana Maharishi, the three states alternate involuntarily for the average man. The last two however, *turiya* and *turyatita* are the results of practice and form clear aids to liberation. Of the three state—*jagrat*, *swapna*, and *sushupti*—each one is exclusive of the other two, and limited by the conditions of time and space. They are therefore unreal.

Our very experience of *jagrat*, and the *swapna* states prove that the consciousness as the self underlies all the five states, remains perfect all along, and witnesses all of them. However, with regard to similar consciousness in deep sleep, every person is known to say 'I was not aware of anything; I slept soundly and happily.' But is there anyone who says, when they wake up, that they slept well? Unless these feelings existed and were experienced in sleep they could not find expressions in the waking state. This leads us to the inference that just as the eye sees the darkness which remains enveloping all objects, so also the self sees the darkness of ignorance which remained covering the phenomenal world.

Ramana describes the state of deep sleep or *sushupti* in a unique manner: 'This darkness is experienced when it (the self) emerged in dots of supreme bliss, shone a trice and fleeted away in such fine subtlety as the rays of the moon which peer through the waving foliage.' The experience was however, not through any media (such as the senses of the mind), but bears out the fact that consciousness does not exist in deep sleep. The unawareness is owing to the absence of relative knowledge, and the happiness to the absence of (seething) thoughts.

If the experience of bliss in deep sleep is a fact, how is it that no one recollects it? 'A diver who has found the desired thing under water,' says Ramana, 'cannot make his discovery known to the expectant persons on the shore until he emerges from the water. Similarly, the sleeper cannot express his experience because he cannot contact the organs of expression until he is awakened by his habits in due course.'

IV. Experience Osho: Your True Nature

Osho (1986) explores the mystic approach to dreams and its relationship to meditation. According to eastern psychology, he says, there are four stages of mind; not just two, as it is according to the western philosophy—the conscious and unconscious mind.

The truth is that the mind has four states: the waking state, which is comparable to the conscious mind; the sleeping state with dreams, which is parallel to the unconscious mind; the dreamless sleep, which the west has yet to find; and the real waking state.

The first is only the so-called waking state, and the fourth is the real awakening. The second is sleep with dreams, but this appears to be a disturbed state. During an eight-hour sleep, you are dreaming for six hours. The remaining two hours belong to the third state, which western psychology does not yet recognize; it has not come across it yet.

Those two hours do not occur in one solid block, but are split into a few minutes here and there. Thus, during eight hours of sleep, you have two hours of the third state—which is dreamless sleep. This is what rejuvenates or revitalizes you.

This is why, at this point, dreams stop, there are no dreams because there is no suppression of thought. Suppression of thought only goes up to the unconscious state, so the dreams remain here. The third stage is deeper than the unconscious; it is unconscious, but far deeper, so that even a dream is not possible.

These two hours are considered the most important because there is no disturbance at all. The body functions naturally. Everything is relaxed and suspended. Time disappears. It is as if you are dead.

It is also the time your sleep gives you rest. If you miss it, in the morning you will feel you have been sleeping—but you actually wake more tired than when you had gone to bed, as if the sleep itself has been tiring. This is because dreams are like worries, which have been picturized.

The third stage is also important because going deeper below it, is the real awakening.

Just before the morning, the night gets very dark. Do not be worried about the darkness. The darker the night gets, the closer the morning is.

The third state is the darkest, the period where you are most unconscious.

If you are a meditator, then you can go from this third stage to the fourth. If you are not a meditator, then from the third you come back to the second, from the second back to the first, and your daily routine goes on. The fourth stage just remains there in the underground, which is your basic reality.

The meditator starts watching from the first stage, the so-called waking stage. Then slowly, he starts watching the second stage—when there are dreams he is also there watching. Now he is not a part of the dreams, he is standing alone and the dreams are on the screen.

As he becomes more skilful in watching, he can slip even deeper, to where there is all darkness, and nothing to watch except the darkness, but it is tremendously peaceful and immensely silent; its depth is unfathomable. As the watcher goes on watching, it becomes darker and darker, thicker and thicker.

This has been called 'the dark night of the soul' by the mystics.

If one becomes afraid—because one has never seen such darkness, experienced such deafening silence, or entered into such an unknown, unfathomable space—one can go back to the second or the first stage.

During this time, one must continue to remember that when the night is the darkest, the morning is very close. These are the moments when the master can be helpful; otherwise it may be a very difficult stage—only a few courageous people enter this stage It is an unknown, endless cave.

If the master is present and he tells you that there is nothing to be afraid of and that this is one of the most restful, most nourishing life giving forces. you can go ahead without any fear.

Suddenly you see the sun rising on the horizon. According to the mystics of all the ages, it is as if thousands of suns are rising all over the horizon; the light is so bright and strong that one cannot believe that it existed under these dark layers of your being.

So when the dreams stop, it is not that repression is working, or that only a little steam is allowed to escape. Rather, you are moving into a third stage which is more important—the second stage is only a passage.

As your meditation grows deeper, the second space disappears because dreaming stops. As your thinking stops in meditation, in sleep your dreaming stops.

Dreaming is like thinking; the difference is that thinking is linguistic and dreaming is pictorial. Dreaming is like the ancient languages, and thinking is like more contemporary languages, but both appear to be the same.

Once you are able, by watching, to stop thinking, you will be able to stop dreaming; then the second stage disappears. From the first stage you can directly enter into the third.

Since thinking and dreaming have stopped, your third stage will not last long either, because your first stage is becoming closer and closer to the fourth—it is becoming thoughtless awareness.

So finally, the second disappears first, then the third and then the first changes its character totally merges with the fourth. Thus only the fourth and last stage remains.

In the east it is called *turiya*. *Turiya* simply means 'the fourth'. It is a number; it is not a name. Although there are names for the other three stages, the fourth stage does not have any name.

All the stages discussed were not part of your nature, they were imposed layers. The fourth you bring with your birth, and when you die you take the fourth with you. The fourth is you. The first three stages were three rings of experiences surrounding you—the fourth is the centre.

It is a different way of saying the same thing: that reaching the fourth stage you become enlightened, or awakened.

Being in the Flow: Tibetan Dream Yoga

According to the Dalai Lama, Tibetan Buddhism considers

sleep to be a form of nourishment, like food, that restores and refreshes the body. He also says that another type of nourishment is *samadhi*, or meditative concentration. If one becomes advanced enough in the practice of meditative concentration, then this itself sustains or nourishes the body.

An interesting way of unfolding the mysteries of the inner process is through dream yoga. A successful seeker in dream work must be stable enough in presence to avoid being swept away by the winds of karmic emotions and lost in the dream. As the mind steadies, dreams become longer, less fragmented, and more easily remembered, and lucidity is developed. Waking life is equally enhanced, as we find that we are increasingly protected from being carried away by the habitual emotional reactions that draw us into distraction and unhappiness. Dream work can instead develop the positive traits that lead to happiness and support the seeker in his spiritual journey.

Tibetan dream yoga teaches us to realize that we are dreaming while having a dream in order to become lucid and to identify with the dream being, the true creator of our experiences. The process of awakening to the reality of dreaming can be facilitated by the means of practising remembrance (remembering and reminding ourselves that we are dreaming during the daytime). Such a practice, called 'Dream being', implies surrendering to the flow of energy and setting ourselves free, a totally natural and spontaneous reaction, which is referred to as 'being in the flow'.

Being aware of the flow of the energy of dreaming brings about a profound sense of freedom, whilst going against the flow usually tends to turn the dream into a nightmare. In order to experience such a degree of freedom, it may be easier to first imagine being in the flow while daydreaming. The practice of dream being requires becoming totally attentive to the flow of daydreaming first. All the other methods and steps in the practice depend on the degree of attention we can focus on the present moment while we engage in dreaming.

The Practices of Tibetan Dream Yoga

It is important to create a spiritual context for the practice of Tibetan dream yoga. Lucid dreaming can easily be misused to perpetuate the problems we experience in our waking lives. For example, one might direct one's dream towards a gratifying encounter or a vengeful fantasy. You will find that the techniques of Tibetan Dream Yoga somehow do not work as well when used for such purposes.

Tibetan dream yoga practice comprises three parts:

1. Daytime practice, designed to help us recognize the dreamlike nature of all existence and thereby prepare us to experience our dreams as vividly as we do our waking activities.

2. Morning wake-up practices that help us recall our dreams, and confirm our determination to recall more of them.
3. Nighttime practice, which prepares the ground for lucid dreaming and spiritual experiences.

Daytime Practice

During the day, practice these four points:

— Contemplating the body as illusory and unreal.

— Contemplating the mind and mental activities as similarly insubstantial.

— Regarding the world and all phenomena and experience as dreamlike, insubstantial, impermanent, and unreal.

— Recognizing the relativity and ungraspable quality such as time, space, knowledge, and awareness.

Reminding ourselves of these four truths throughout our waking hours helps to dissolve the barrier between the dream of life and the sleeping dream. As we become more adept at these practices, we begin to regard our nighttime dreams as continuations of our waking dream and we learn how to bring habitual awareness to both.

Mirror Practice

The following mirror practice is an effective way of perceiving the dreamlike nature of 'reality' and especially of 'self'. From time to time during the day, take a few minutes to do this exercise:

1. Stand in front of a mirror and look into your eyes.
2. Hold up a hand mirror behind your right or left ear and look at its reflection in the larger mirror. Keep angling the hand mirror so as to fragment and multiply your image as much as possible. Let your mind fragment along with the image.
3. After a few minutes, angle the hand mirror back until you return to the original, single image in the mirror in front of you.

The analogy of a mirror image is, like dreams, traditionally used to describe the insubstantial nature of our everyday experience. The mirror practice helps bring that teaching to life. The fragmented image is the kind we might see in a dream; yet we are seeing it while we're fully awake—or are we?

Allowing your mind to 'fall apart' also helps ventilate the solidity we typically attribute to our world, and especially to our 'self'.

Partner Exercise

Here is a traditional dream yoga practice you can do with a partner. This is an immensely useful technique, not only to challenge the distinction between sleeping dreams and the dream of being awake, but also for applying your training to practical, everyday situations.

1. Insult, blame, and criticize your partner. Your partner should listen to all of this as echoes—empty sounds.
2. Trade places. Now have your partner disparage you, while you practise just hearing the sounds and not taking the words to heart.
3. Try doing this same exercise using praise and flattery instead of blame.

In either case, the listening partner should practise not reacting in any way, recognizing what is being said as a dream. At first, you may find it difficult to maintain equanimity while you do this practice. Stay with it—you will find that doing so yields rich rewards over time.

Nighttime Practice

After going to bed, practice these four points in order to create the conditions for mindful, lucid dreaming.

1. Chant the following prayer three times to remind you of and strengthen your resolve to awaken within the dream, for the benefit of the ultimate awakening of all beings: 'May I awaken within this dream and grasp the fact that I am dreaming, so that all dreamlike beings may likewise awaken from the nightmare of illusory suffering and confusion.'

2. Lie on one side with your legs together and knees slightly bent. Let your bent arm take the weight of your torso by resting your head on your open hand. This is the posture of the sleeping Buddha, as he has been traditionally depicted at the moment of passing into *nirvana*.
3. Bringing your attention to your throat *chakra*, visualize your energy rising up out of your body. Feel it rise up from your heart *chakra* with your breath and pass into your 'third eye' or brow *chakra*: the point between your eyebrows. Visualize it as a full, luminous moon behind your eyes. Go into the light.
4. Visualize the letter A (symbolizing infinite space) on the surface of the moon.
5. Notice whatever images begin to appear on the sphere of light behind your eyes.

Tibetan dream yoga is dedicated to helping dreamwork gain a powerful and central place in our interconnected, high-energy world culture. Its practitioners believe that humanity requires more than waking wisdom in order to successfully steer through the obstacles that lie ahead of us in the new millennium. There exists within you a wisdom, a compassion, a divine plan that can heal, guide, and protect, if you will simply take the time to learn how to listen and cooperate with it.

Images on the Sufi Path

Dreams, Sufis say, speaking of 'true dreams' (*ar-ru'yâ as-sâliha*), are symbolic messages which arise from the knowledge hidden in the centre of being. In the wilderness of the unknown through which the seeker travels, these encoded messages give a forecast and a foretaste of things to come.

Not all dreams are 'true dreams'; most dreams are spun, Sufis say, by the needs of the lower self, or by the mind churning the events of the day. Such dreams are usually confused and fragmented, and are characteristically called 'dreams in confusion' (*adghâth al-ahlâm*). Occasionally, there appears a dream, or a series of dreams, which bears the hallmark of true knowledge, a knowledge which, though concealed from the mind and the body's sense perception, responds directly and instructively to the true needs of the dreamer's soul. Such dreams often have an aura of luminosity which doesn't require interpretation. Their meaning looms clear on the inner horizon. They have a feeling quality which touches the dreamer and awakens in him dormant emotions, perceptions, a new insight into the direction his life is taking. The dreamer, if he is sincere in his quest for truth and meaning, will listen, understand, and respond to the inner taskmaster who reveals himself in the dream, and who knows him better than he knows himself.

This 'inner consistency, coherence, and intelligence' is that which knows in spite of the outer unknown. When it unmasks itself in a dream, it often becomes the seeker's only confirmation and support, especially in periods of anguish, loss of direction, and despair. Yet in order to become realized in life, it demands of the dreamer attentiveness and trust. To trust the message inherent in the dream means to be prepared to go through the inner and outer changes which it heralds.

The Sufi Mystic Bawa Muhaiyadden (Hixon, n.d.) declares that all objects and structures are projected by the mind and exist only for the collective mind of sentient beings. He presents this insight by pointing out the essential similarity between waking and a dream, a similarity that is not simply metaphorical but reflects the fundamental nature of all phenomena as consciousness. The only difference between waking and dreaming is that the waking state constitutes a collective dream, continually and roughly agreed upon by all conscious beings, whereas the dream state is subjective, or private to each individual centre of consciousness.

Sleeping and waking dreams are not fundamentally different: they both exist as mental projections. Yet Bawa counsels us to take the waking dream seriously: to be careful with all lives, to regard all suffering as our own, and to observe precisely all phenomena, tracing them to their ultimate source in Allah. Thus, we learn to manifest more and more clearly the attributes of God such as justice, compassion, and wisdom. Our learning to become transparent to the Divine, expressing more and more clearly the divine attributes, is the purpose of this collective dream we call the universe and which is actually, God dreaming through us.

Entering ecstasy, Bawa now reveals that God and the divine attributes alone truly exist, that both subjective dreams and the cosmic dream are ultimately unreal, appearing only provisionally as a teaching for souls.

The dreams seen at night and the dreams seen during the day are the actors. But they will have to end their acts, they will have to take off their make-up and some day show their true forms. Then they know their original form.

All forms are masks of God. All sentient beings express the pure consciousness and power that is God. When they remove their masks, they will know their original form, which is, paradoxically, without form or structure.

References

Balsekar, S. Ramesh, Wayne Liquorman. 1992. *Consciousness Speaks: Conversations with Ramesh S. Balsekar*. Advaita Press.

Barbach, Lonnie G. Dr. 1987. *Erotic Interludes: Editor of Pleasures*. Harper Collins Publishers, Toronto.

Boss, Medard. 1958. *The Analysis of Dreams*. Philosophical Library. New York.

Delaney, Gayle. 1991. *Breakthrough Dreaming: How to tap the power of your 24 hour mind*. Bantam Books.

Delaney, Gayle. 1994. *Sexual Dreams*. Ballantine Books.

Delaney, Gayle. 1979. *Living Your Dreams*. Harper, San Francisco.

Freud, Sigmund. 1976. *The Interpretation of Dreams*. Penguin Books.

Gackenbach, Jayne and Jane Bosveld. 1989. *Control Your Dreams*. Harper and Row, New York.

Garfield, Patricia. 1991. *The Healing Power of Dreams*. Simon and Schuster.

Gates, Donald. 1971. *Elmer Gates and the Art of Mind-Using*. Exposition Press.

Hall, S. Calvin and Robert L. Van der Castle. 1966. *The Contemporary Analysis of Dreams*. Appleton-Century Crofts.

Hall, S. Calvin. 1953. *The Meaning of Dreams*. McGraw Hill.

Hall, S. Calvin. 1966. *The Meaning of Dreams*. McGraw Hill Paperback.

Hartmann, Ernest. 1973. *The Functions of Sleep*. Yale University Press.

Horney, Karen. 1964. *The Neurotic Personality of Our Time*. W.W. Norton & Company.

Jethmalani, Sangeeta. 1993. *Experiment on Dreams and Color Puncture*. Tentative Findings reported at Seminar on Color Puncture. Tata Management Training Centre.

Kaplan-Williams, Strephon. 1986. *The Jungian-Senoi Dreamwork Manual*. Journey Press.

Koestler, Arthur, 1959. *The Sleep Walkrs*. MacMillan.

Laberge, Stephen. 1985. *Lucid Dreaming*. Jeremy P. Tacher.

Maharishi, Sri Ramana. 1989. *Talks With Sri Ramana Maharishi*. Sri Ramanasramam.

Master, Farokh. 1999. *Homeopathic Dictionary of Dreams* B. Jain Publisher, New Delhi.

Maury L.F.A. 1853. 'Nouvelles observations sur les analogies des phenomenes du reve et de alienation mental'. Pt.II Ann. *Med-psychology.*

Menezes, Francis, 1989, *Time in Dreams*. Paper presented at International Seminar on 'TIME' organized by Tata Institute of Fundamental Research and Max Mueller Bhavan at Bombay.

Menezes, Francis A. 1993. Paper on '*Dreamwork In Management Training*'. Global Management Development Forum. Stiges, Spain.

Nikhilananda, Swami. 1987. Translator and Annotator. *The Mandukyopanisad*. Advaita Ashrama.

Norbu, Namkhai. 1992, *Dream Yoga and the Practice of Natural Light*. Snow Lion Publications.

Osho, 1986. *The Transmission of the Lamp*. Osho International Foundation.

Perls, S. Fredrick. 1969. *Gestalt Therapy Verbatim*. Real People Press.

Reed, Henry. 1994. *Getting Help From Your Dreams*. Ballantine Books.

Rogers, Carl. 1961. *On Becoming a Person*. Houghton, Mifflin.

Rossi, Ernest. 1988. *The Psychobiology of Mind-Body Healing*. Norton, New York.

Satyananda, Swami Sarawati. 1976. *Yoga Nidra*. Bihar School of Yoga, Munger.

Sri Aurobindo and the Mother. 1971. *Sleep and Dreams*. Sri Aurobindo Ashram Trust.

Stevens, John O. (ed.) 1975. *Gestalt Is*. Real People Press.

Stevenson, Robert Louis. 1892. *Across the Plains*. Windus, Picadilly, London.

The Holy Bible. 1957. *Burns and Oates*, Macmillan & Co. Ltd.

Ullman, Montague, Krippner, Stanley & Vaughan, Alan. 1988. *Dream Telepathy*. McFarland Press.

Ullman, Montague and Nan Zimmerman. 1970. *Working With Dreams*. Jeremy P. Tacher.

Vaughan-Lee, Llewellyn. 1992. *The Call & The Echo*. Threshold Books.

Notes

Notes

Notes